The WEDDING PLANNER

by
Martha Stewart

PHOTOGRAPHS BY CHRISTOPHER BAKER

Clarkson N. Potter, Inc./Publishers

Published by Clarkson N. Potter, Inc., 201 East 50th Street, New York, New York 10022,
and distributed by Crown Publishers, Inc.

CLARKSON N. POTTER, POTTER, and colophon are trademarks of Clarkson N. Potter, Inc.

Design by Jan Melchior, with inspiration from Ellen Burnie

Manufactured in Japan
Library of Congress Cataloging-in-Publication Data
Stewart, Martha.
[Wedding planner]
The wedding planner / by Martha Stewart; photographs by Christopher Baker.
p. cm.
1. Weddings—United States—Planning—Handbooks, manuals, etc.
2. Marriage customs and rites—United States—Handbooks, manuals, etc.
I. Baker, Christopher. II. Title. III. Title: Wedding planner.
GT2703.S74 1988
392′.5—dc19
88-9777
CIP
ISBN 0-517-56566-8
10 9 8 7 6 5 4 3

Introduction

Ever since I first began catering weddings, I have been very interested in the organization and planning of the wedding day. I was always curious to observe the methods by which my clients kept their records, filed their fabric samples, and maintained the voluminous quantity of information that accumulates when one plans such a complicated event.

Some brides had magnificent systems of notebooks and files that listed complete details, others just an envelope into which everything was tossed for later sorting. Some started with one or more of the "planners" available on the market, but soon found them inadequate.

As my business developed from straight catering into a more full-service wedding consultancy, I began to formulate my own organization notebook. I gradually created one basic book that worked for each of the weddings we were involved in. I tried to condense contracts and lists into the essence of each subject. I tried to make things as clear and simple as possible for our staff, for the bride, and for everyone else involved in the wedding. The planner you hold in your hands is based on the book I designed for myself.

There are many things to consider when planning one's wedding, and we have addressed each and every one of them in this planner. Each section has been arranged to provide adequate space for record keeping, cross-referencing, filing, and notes. There are special pockets for keeping copies of contracts, cards, receipts, and color and fabric samples. There are checklists, calendars, a diary, and itemized lists of "Things to Remember," all those tiny details that make each wedding perfect. There are hints and tips; we have even included grid paper to make the plotting of seating plans and table arrangements easier. For inspiration and reference, there are one hundred full-color photographs highlighting all aspects of the wedding day.

This wedding planner is the result of more than twelve years of planning and organizing weddings. We hope that each and every section will aid the bride, her family, and her attendants in the creation of a very special occasion. And we hope that the completed planner, when once used to its fullest, will ensure the bride and groom a record of all that went into the formation of one of the most important days of their lives.

Calendar and Planner

Calendar

THINGS TO REMEMBER

As your wedding day approaches, demands on your time will be great. On the following pages we give you a personal calendar where you can fill in appointments month by month, week by week, and finally, hour by hour.

Your first decision will be to choose the date of your wedding. It takes at least six months to plan a formal wedding (often longer) and at least three to four months to plan an informal wedding. Be sure to set your wedding date far enough ahead so you won't have to settle for second choices in ceremony and reception locations, musicians, and other details.

Consider where the holidays fall when planning your wedding date; a three-day weekend may be useful for guests coming from out of town, but inconvenient for others.

Remember daylight savings time—you may find that your wedding is taking place in the dark when you had expected gentle twilight. (If you choose a change-over weekend, be sure to alert all participants, and confirm all appointments and times.)

Keep your own monthly calendar in mind when scheduling the wedding date and honeymoon.

Try to avoid conflicts with other family members' special events: birthdays, anniversaries, graduations, and other occasions.

1989

JANUARY

S	M	T	W	T	F	S
1	2	3	4	5	6	7
8	9	10	11	12	13	14
15	16	17	18	19	20	21
22	23	24	25	26	27	28
29	30	31				

FEBRUARY

S	M	T	W	T	F	S
			1	2	3	4
5	6	7	8	9	10	11
12	13	14	15	16	17	18
19	20	21	22	23	24	25
26	27	28				

MARCH

S	M	T	W	T	F	S
			1	2	3	4
5	6	7	8	9	10	11
12	13	14	15	16	17	18
19	20	21	22	23	24	25
26	27	28	29	30	31	

APRIL

S	M	T	W	T	F	S
						1
2	3	4	5	6	7	8
9	10	11	12	13	14	15
16	17	18	19	20	21	22
23	24	25	26	27	28	29
30						

MAY

S	M	T	W	T	F	S
	1	2	3	4	5	6
7	8	9	10	11	12	13
14	15	16	17	18	19	20
21	22	23	24	25	26	27
28	29	30	31			

JUNE

S	M	T	W	T	F	S
				1	2	3
4	5	6	7	8	9	10
11	12	13	14	15	16	17
18	19	20	21	22	23	24
25	26	27	28	29	30	

JULY

S	M	T	W	T	F	S
						1
2	3	4	5	6	7	8
9	10	11	12	13	14	15
16	17	18	19	20	21	22
23	24	25	26	27	28	29
30	31					

AUGUST

S	M	T	W	T	F	S
		1	2	3	4	5
6	7	8	9	10	11	12
13	14	15	16	17	18	19
20	21	22	23	24	25	26
27	28	29	30	31		

SEPTEMBER

S	M	T	W	T	F	S
					1	2
3	4	5	6	7	8	9
10	11	12	13	14	15	16
17	18	19	20	21	22	23
24	25	26	27	28	29	30

OCTOBER

S	M	T	W	T	F	S
1	2	3	4	5	6	7
8	9	10	11	12	13	14
15	16	17	18	19	20	21
22	23	24	25	26	27	28
29	30	31				

NOVEMBER

S	M	T	W	T	F	S
			1	2	3	4
5	6	7	8	9	10	11
12	13	14	15	16	17	18
19	20	21	22	23	24	25
26	27	28	29	30		

DECEMBER

S	M	T	W	T	F	S
					1	2
3	4	5	6	7	8	9
10	11	12	13	14	15	16
17	18	19	20	21	22	23
24	25	26	27	28	29	30
31						

1989 HOLIDAYS

Sunday, January 1—New Year's Day
Monday, January 16—Martin Luther King, Jr.'s birthday observed
Monday, February 20—Washington's birthday observed
Sunday, March 26—Easter
Thursday, April 20—1st day of Passover
Monday, May 29—Memorial Day observed
Tuesday, July 4—Independence Day
Monday, September 4—Labor Day
Saturday, September 30—1st day of Rosh Hashana
Monday, October 9—Yom Kippur; Columbus Day observed
Thursday, November 23—Thanksgiving
Saturday, December 23—1st day of Hanukkah
Monday, December 25—Christmas

1990

JANUARY

S	M	T	W	T	F	S
	1	2	3	4	5	6
7	8	9	10	11	12	13
14	15	16	17	18	19	20
21	22	23	24	25	26	27
28	29	30	31			

FEBRUARY

S	M	T	W	T	F	S
				1	2	3
4	5	6	7	8	9	10
11	12	13	14	15	16	17
18	19	20	21	22	23	24
25	26	27	28			

MARCH

S	M	T	W	T	F	S
				1	2	3
4	5	6	7	8	9	10
11	12	13	14	15	16	17
18	19	20	21	22	23	24
25	26	27	28	29	30	31

APRIL

S	M	T	W	T	F	S
1	2	3	4	5	6	7
8	9	10	11	12	13	14
15	16	17	18	19	20	21
22	23	24	25	26	27	28
29	30					

MAY

S	M	T	W	T	F	S
		1	2	3	4	5
6	7	8	9	10	11	12
13	14	15	16	17	18	19
20	21	22	23	24	25	26
27	28	29	30	31		

JUNE

S	M	T	W	T	F	S
					1	2
3	4	5	6	7	8	9
10	11	12	13	14	15	16
17	18	19	20	21	22	23
24	25	26	27	28	29	30

JULY

S	M	T	W	T	F	S
1	2	3	4	5	6	7
8	9	10	11	12	13	14
15	16	17	18	19	20	21
22	23	24	25	26	27	28
29	30	31				

AUGUST

S	M	T	W	T	F	S
			1	2	3	4
5	6	7	8	9	10	11
12	13	14	15	16	17	18
19	20	21	22	23	24	25
26	27	28	29	30	31	

SEPTEMBER

S	M	T	W	T	F	S
						1
2	3	4	5	6	7	8
9	10	11	12	13	14	15
16	17	18	19	20	21	22
23	24	25	26	27	28	29
30						

OCTOBER

S	M	T	W	T	F	S
	1	2	3	4	5	6
7	8	9	10	11	12	13
14	15	16	17	18	19	20
21	22	23	24	25	26	27
28	29	30	31			

NOVEMBER

S	M	T	W	T	F	S
				1	2	3
4	5	6	7	8	9	10
11	12	13	14	15	16	17
18	19	20	21	22	23	24
25	26	27	28	29	30	

DECEMBER

S	M	T	W	T	F	S
						1
2	3	4	5	6	7	8
9	10	11	12	13	14	15
16	17	18	19	20	21	22
23	24	25	26	27	28	29
30	31					

1990 HOLIDAYS

Monday, January 1—New Year's Day
Monday, January 15—Martin Luther King, Jr.'s birthday observed
Monday, February 19—Washington's birthday observed
Tuesday, April 10—1st day of Passover
Sunday, April 15—Easter
Monday, May 28—Memorial Day observed
Wednesday, July 4—Independence Day
Monday, September 3—Labor Day
Thursday, September 20—1st day of Rosh Hashana
Saturday, September 29—Yom Kippur
Monday, October 8—Columbus Day observed
Thursday, November 22—Thanksgiving
Wednesday, December 12—1st day of Hanukkah
Tuesday, December 25—Christmas

1991

JANUARY

S	M	T	W	T	F	S
		1	2	3	4	5
6	7	8	9	10	11	12
13	14	15	16	17	18	19
20	21	22	23	24	25	26
27	28	29	30	31		

FEBRUARY

S	M	T	W	T	F	S
					1	2
3	4	5	6	7	8	9
10	11	12	13	14	15	16
17	18	19	20	21	22	23
24	25	26	27	28		

MARCH

S	M	T	W	T	F	S
					1	2
3	4	5	6	7	8	9
10	11	12	13	14	15	16
17	18	19	20	21	22	23
24	25	26	27	28	29	30
31						

APRIL

S	M	T	W	T	F	S
	1	2	3	4	5	6
7	8	9	10	11	12	13
14	15	16	17	18	19	20
21	22	23	24	25	26	27
28	29	30				

MAY

S	M	T	W	T	F	S
			1	2	3	4
5	6	7	8	9	10	11
12	13	14	15	16	17	18
19	20	21	22	23	24	25
26	27	28	29	30	31	

JUNE

S	M	T	W	T	F	S
						1
2	3	4	5	6	7	8
9	10	11	12	13	14	15
16	17	18	19	20	21	22
23	24	25	26	27	28	29
30						

JULY

S	M	T	W	T	F	S
	1	2	3	4	5	6
7	8	9	10	11	12	13
14	15	16	17	18	19	20
21	22	23	24	25	26	27
28	29	30	31			

AUGUST

S	M	T	W	T	F	S
				1	2	3
4	5	6	7	8	9	10
11	12	13	14	15	16	17
18	19	20	21	22	23	24
25	26	27	28	29	30	31

SEPTEMBER

S	M	T	W	T	F	S
1	2	3	4	5	6	7
8	9	10	11	12	13	14
15	16	17	18	19	20	21
22	23	24	25	26	27	28
29	30					

OCTOBER

S	M	T	W	T	F	S
		1	2	3	4	5
6	7	8	9	10	11	12
13	14	15	16	17	18	19
20	21	22	23	24	25	26
27	28	29	30	31		

NOVEMBER

S	M	T	W	T	F	S
					1	2
3	4	5	6	7	8	9
10	11	12	13	14	15	16
17	18	19	20	21	22	23
24	25	26	27	28	29	30

DECEMBER

S	M	T	W	T	F	S
1	2	3	4	5	6	7
8	9	10	11	12	13	14
15	16	17	18	19	20	21
22	23	24	25	26	27	28
29	30	31				

1991 HOLIDAYS

Tuesday, January 1—New Year's Day

Monday, January 21—Martin Luther King, Jr.'s birthday observed

Monday, February 18—Washington's birthday observed

Saturday, March 30—1st day of Passover

Sunday, March 31—Easter

Monday, May 27—Memorial Day observed

Thursday, July 4—Independence Day

Monday, September 2—Labor Day

Monday, September 9—1st day of Rosh Hashana

Wednesday, September 18—Yom Kippur

Monday, October 14—Columbus Day observed

Thursday, November 28—Thanksgiving

Monday, December 2—1st day of Hanukkah

Wednesday, December 25—Christmas

1992

JANUARY

S	M	T	W	T	F	S
			1	2	3	4
5	6	7	8	9	10	11
12	13	14	15	16	17	18
19	20	21	22	23	24	25
26	27	28	29	30	31	

FEBRUARY

S	M	T	W	T	F	S
						1
2	3	4	5	6	7	8
9	10	11	12	13	14	15
16	17	18	19	20	21	22
23	24	25	26	27	28	29

MARCH

S	M	T	W	T	F	S
1	2	3	4	5	6	7
8	9	10	11	12	13	14
15	16	17	18	19	20	21
22	23	24	25	26	27	28
29	30	31				

APRIL

S	M	T	W	T	F	S
			1	2	3	4
5	6	7	8	9	10	11
12	13	14	15	16	17	18
19	20	21	22	23	24	25
26	27	28	29	30		

MAY

S	M	T	W	T	F	S
					1	2
3	4	5	6	7	8	9
10	11	12	13	14	15	16
17	18	19	20	21	22	23
24	25	26	27	28	29	30
31						

JUNE

S	M	T	W	T	F	S
	1	2	3	4	5	6
7	8	9	10	11	12	13
14	15	16	17	18	19	20
21	22	23	24	25	26	27
28	29	30				

JULY

S	M	T	W	T	F	S
			1	2	3	4
5	6	7	8	9	10	11
12	13	14	15	16	17	18
19	20	21	22	23	24	25
26	27	28	29	30	31	

AUGUST

S	M	T	W	T	F	S
						1
2	3	4	5	6	7	8
9	10	11	12	13	14	15
16	17	18	19	20	21	22
23	24	25	26	27	28	29
30	31					

SEPTEMBER

S	M	T	W	T	F	S
		1	2	3	4	5
6	7	8	9	10	11	12
13	14	15	16	17	18	19
20	21	22	23	24	25	26
27	28	29	30			

OCTOBER

S	M	T	W	T	F	S
				1	2	3
4	5	6	7	8	9	10
11	12	13	14	15	16	17
18	19	20	21	22	23	24
25	26	27	28	29	30	31

NOVEMBER

S	M	T	W	T	F	S
1	2	3	4	5	6	7
8	9	10	11	12	13	14
15	16	17	18	19	20	21
22	23	24	25	26	27	28
29	30					

DECEMBER

S	M	T	W	T	F	S
		1	2	3	4	5
6	7	8	9	10	11	12
13	14	15	16	17	18	19
20	21	22	23	24	25	26
27	28	29	30	31		

1992 HOLIDAYS

Wednesday, January 1—New Year's Day

Monday, January 20—Martin Luther King, Jr.'s birthday observed

Monday, February 17—Washington's birthday observed

Saturday, April 18—1st day of Passover

Sunday, April 19—Easter

Monday, May 25—Memorial Day observed

Saturday, July 4—Independence Day

Monday, September 7—Labor Day

Monday, September 28—1st day of Rosh Hashana

Wednesday, October 7—Yom Kippur

Monday, October 12—Columbus Day observed

Thursday, November 26—Thanksgiving

Sunday, December 20—1st day of Hanukkah

Friday, December 25—Christmas

Month of . . . .

SIX MONTHS BEFORE WEDDING

1 . . . .
2 . . . .
3 . . . .
4 . . . .
5 . . . .
6 . . . .
7 . . . .
8 . . . .
9 . . . .
10 . . . .
11 . . . .
12 . . . .
13 . . . .
14 . . . .
15 . . . .
16 . . . .
17 . . . .
18 . . . .
19 . . . .
20 . . . .
21 . . . .
22 . . . .
23 . . . .
24 . . . .
25 . . . .
26 . . . .
27 . . . .
28 . . . .
29 . . . .
30 . . . .
31 . . . .

Month of . . . .

FIVE MONTHS BEFORE WEDDING

1 . . . .
2 . . . .
3 . . . .
4 . . . .
5 . . . .
6 . . . .
7 . . . .
8 . . . .
9 . . . .
10 . . . .
11 . . . .
12 . . . .
13 . . . .
14 . . . .
15 . . . .
16 . . . .
17 . . . .
18 . . . .
19 . . . .
20 . . . .
21 . . . .
22 . . . .
23 . . . .
24 . . . .
25 . . . .
26 . . . .
27 . . . .
28 . . . .
29 . . . .
30 . . . .
31 . . . .

Month of . . . .

FOUR MONTHS BEFORE WEDDING

1 . . . .

2 . . . .

3 . . . .

4 . . . .

5 . . . .

6 . . . .

7 . . . .

8 . . . .

9 . . . .

10 . . . .

11 . . . .

12 . . . .

13 . . . .

14 . . . .

15 . . . .

16 . . . .

17 . . . .

18 . . . .

19 . . . .

20 . . . .

21 . . . .

22 . . . .

23 . . . .

24 . . . .

25 . . . .

26 . . . .

27 . . . .

28 . . . .

29 . . . .

30 . . . .

31 . . . .

Month of . . . .

THREE MONTHS BEFORE WEDDING

1 . . . .

2 . . . .

3 . . . .

4 . . . .

5 . . . .

6 . . . .

7 . . . .

8 . . . .

9 . . . .

10 . . . .

11 . . . .

12 . . . .

13 . . . .

14 . . . .

15 . . . .

16 . . . .

17 . . . .

18 . . . .

19 . . . .

20 . . . .

21 . . . .

22 . . . .

23 . . . .

24 . . . .

25 . . . .

26 . . . .

27 . . . .

28 . . . .

29 . . . .

30 . . . .

31 . . . .

Week of . . . .

EIGHT WEEKS BEFORE WEDDING

MONDAY

TUESDAY

WEDNESDAY

THURSDAY

FRIDAY

SATURDAY

SUNDAY

Week of . . . .

SEVEN WEEKS BEFORE WEDDING

MONDAY

TUESDAY

WEDNESDAY

THURSDAY

FRIDAY

SATURDAY

SUNDAY

Week of . . . .

SIX WEEKS BEFORE WEDDING

MONDAY

TUESDAY

WEDNESDAY

THURSDAY

FRIDAY

SATURDAY

SUNDAY

Week of . . . .

FIVE WEEKS BEFORE WEDDING

MONDAY

TUESDAY

WEDNESDAY

THURSDAY

FRIDAY

SATURDAY

SUNDAY

Week of . . . .

FOUR WEEKS BEFORE WEDDING

MONDAY

TUESDAY

WEDNESDAY

THURSDAY

FRIDAY

SATURDAY

SUNDAY

Week of . . . .

THREE WEEKS BEFORE WEDDING

MONDAY

TUESDAY

WEDNESDAY

THURSDAY

FRIDAY

SATURDAY

SUNDAY

Week of . . . .

TWO WEEKS BEFORE WEDDING

MONDAY

TUESDAY

WEDNESDAY

THURSDAY

FRIDAY

SATURDAY

SUNDAY

Week of . . . .

ONE WEEK BEFORE WEDDING

MONDAY

TUESDAY

WEDNESDAY

THURSDAY

FRIDAY

SATURDAY

SUNDAY

The Day Before

6:00 A.M. ....

7:00 A.M. ....

8:00 A.M. ....

9:00 A.M. ....

10:00 A.M. ....

11:00 A.M. ....

Noon ....

1:00 P.M. ....

2:00 P.M. ....

3:00 P.M. ....

4:00 P.M. ....

5:00 P.M. ....

6:00 P.M. ....

7:00 P.M. ....

8:00 P.M. ....

9:00 P.M. ....

10:00 P.M. ....

11:00 P.M. ....

Midnight ....

LAUNCH
CLOSED
BY OWNER
WEEK OF JULY 29 -AUG. 5
DUE TO WEDDING

SEA
TRANSPORTATION
AND
CLEANUP

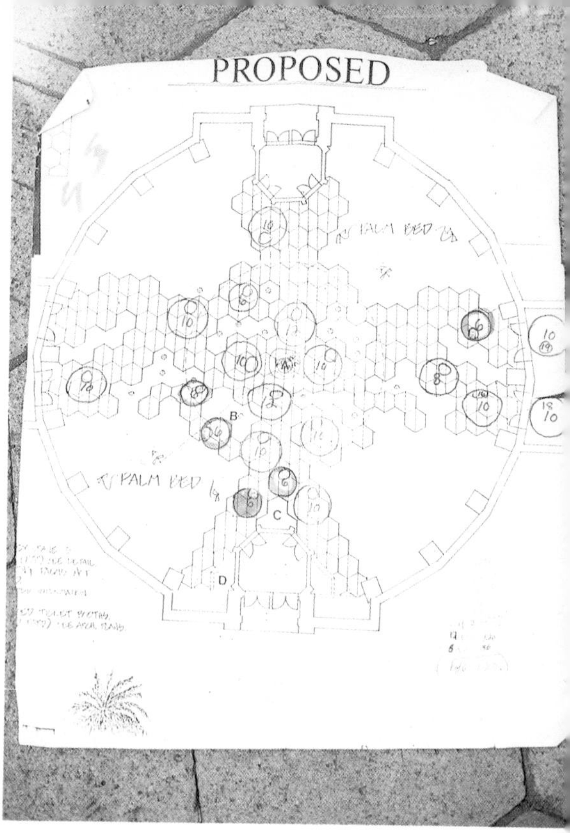

PROPOSED
PALM BED
PALM BED

Planner

Things to Remember

Once you have chosen the date and time of your wedding, make the other basic decisions: budget, location of ceremony and reception; guest list, cleric or judge, and the size of the wedding party.

Caterer and menu

Baker for wedding cake

Bouquets, boutonnieres, and corsages; flowers for church and reception

Music for ceremony and for reception

Tent and lighting equipment, if necessary

Wedding dress, shoes, accessories, and lingerie; garter; bridesmaids' attire

Groom's, groomsmen's and ushers' attire

Invitations and other stationery

Photographer and/or video crew; formal wedding portrait; wedding announcement for newspapers

Wedding rings

Gift registry

Gifts for bride's and groom's attendants

Marriage license (and required medical examinations and tests)

Name change on official documents

Lodging for attendants and out-of-town guests

Rehearsal and rehearsal dinner

Seating plans for rehearsal dinner and reception

Hair, manicure, and facial appointments

Transportation to and from ceremony and reception

Receiving line; guest book and pen

Rice, rose petals, or birdseed to throw

Trousseau; honeymoon plans

The old, new, borrowed, and blue

THE BUDGET

Soon after you become engaged, you will need to discuss and set a budget with your parents, your fiancé, his family, or whomever else is involved. This budget will help you shape the wedding day—dictating the number of guests, type of reception, menu, entertainment, and other elements. The itemized list below will help you project the costs of each element. *This inventory, however, is based on traditional financial responsibilities and should be altered as needed.* For example, it is not uncommon today for the bride and groom themselves to assume all financial obligations.

BRIDE/BRIDE'S FAMILY	ESTIMATED COST	ACTUAL COST
All ceremony costs: location, music, rentals, etc.	....	....
All reception costs: location, food and beverages, entertainment, decorations, etc.	....	....
Wedding dress and accessories	....	....
Trousseau	....	....
Invitations and other stationery, mailing costs	....	....
Bouquets for bridesmaids	....	....
Boutonniere for groom	....	....
Flowers for ceremony and reception	....	....
Party for bridesmaids	....	....
Gifts for groom's and bride's attendants	....	....
Groom's ring	....	....
Blood test, physical exam	....	....
Photography and/or video	....	....

	ESTIMATED COST	ACTUAL COST
Transportation to and from ceremony and reception		
Lodging for bride's out-of-town attendants		

GROOM/GROOM'S FAMILY

	ESTIMATED COST	ACTUAL COST
Bride's engagement and wedding rings		
Groom's wedding attire		
Marriage license		
Cleric's or judge's fee		
Bride's bouquet, boutonnieres for groomsmen, corsages for mothers		
Gifts for bride, best man, and groomsmen		
Blood test, physical exam		
Lodging for groom's out-of-town attendants		
Rehearsal dinner		
Honeymoon		

NEWSPAPER ANNOUNCEMENTS

Check with any publications you would like to have carry an announcement—of the engagement and/or wedding—about their requirements. Remember that if you want your wedding announcement to be accompanied by a photograph, you must send the newspaper a portrait, showing the bride in full wedding dress, several weeks before the actual event.

. . . .

Publication . . . .
. . . .
. . . .
Contact . . . .
Phone (   ). . . . .
Deadline . . . .
Photo . . . .
Sent . . . .
Notes . . . .
. . . .
. . . .
. . . .
. . . .

Publication . . . .
. . . .
. . . .
Contact . . . .
Phone (   ). . . . .
Deadline . . . .
Photo . . . .
Sent . . . .
Notes . . . .
. . . .
. . . .
. . . .
. . . .

Publication . . . .
. . . .
. . . .
Contact . . . .
Phone (   ). . . . .
Deadline . . . .
Photo . . . .
Sent . . . .
Notes . . . .
. . . .
. . . .
. . . .
. . . .

Publication . . . .
. . . .
. . . .
Contact . . . .
Phone (   ). . . . .
Deadline . . . .
Photo . . . .
Sent . . . .
Notes . . . .
. . . .
. . . .
. . . .
. . . .

THE WEDDING PARTY

The following pages are allotted to the members of your wedding party. These pages will provide easy access to addresses and phone numbers which you will undoubtedly need while planning your wedding. You should also use these pages to note any duties you would like particular individuals to take care of (the more traditional ones are listed below) and to indicate parties and events they should attend, such as showers and fittings. Copy and distribute each person's sheet to avoid any confusion or misunderstanding.

It might also be helpful to have a one-page list of all the members of the wedding party (including parents), with addresses and phone numbers. Give the list to people who are planning prenuptial parties, and to each of the attendants, in case they need to get in touch with one another.

Traditional Responsibilities

MAID/MATRON OF HONOR

Helps bride dress for ceremony

Organizes other attendants

Attends all prenuptial parties

Arranges the bride's train and veil

Holds the groom's ring and the bride's bouquet during ceremony

Helps bride dress for the honeymoon

May also help the bride choose her dress, run errands, and record wedding gifts

BRIDESMAIDS

Make themselves available to help the bride and her family with any problems

BEST MAN

Helps groom dress for ceremony

Organizes groomsmen and ushers

Holds bride's ring during ceremony

Handles honeymoon details, such as luggage and tickets, and sees to it that the couple gets away in time

GROOMSMEN/USHERS

Escort guests to their seats at ceremony

Make themselves available to help guests with any problems (parking, directions, etc.) at ceremony and reception

MAID/MATRON OF HONOR

Address ....

....

....

Phone (home) (   ) ....   (work) (   ) ....

Responsibilities ....

....

....

....

....

....

Parties/events to attend ....

....

....

....

....

....

Travel/arrival plans ....

....

....

Lodging ....

....

....

Notes ....

....

....

....

....

....

....

. . . .

BEST MAN

Address . . . .

. . . .

. . . .

Phone (home) (   ) . . . .   (work) (   ) . . . .

Responsibilities . . . .

. . . .

. . . .

. . . .

. . . .

. . . .

Parties/events to attend . . . .

. . . .

. . . .

. . . .

. . . .

. . . .

Travel/arrival plans . . . .

. . . .

. . . .

Lodging . . . .

. . . .

. . . .

Notes . . . .

. . . .

. . . .

. . . .

. . . .

. . . .

. . . .

. . . .

BRIDESMAID

Address . . . .

. . . .

Phone (home) ( ) . . . . (work) ( ) . . . .

Responsibilities . . . .

. . . .

Parties/events to attend . . . .

. . . .

Travel/arrival plans . . . .

. . . .

Lodging . . . .

. . . .

. . . .

BRIDESMAID

Address . . . .

. . . .

Phone (home) ( ) . . . . (work) ( ) . . . .

Responsibilities . . . .

. . . .

Parties/events to attend . . . .

. . . .

Travel/arrival plans . . . .

. . . .

Lodging . . . .

. . . .

. . . .

BRIDESMAID

Address . . . .

Phone (home) (   ) . . . . (work) (   ) . . . .

Responsibilities . . . .

Parties/events to attend . . . .

Travel/arrival plans . . . .

Lodging . . . .

. . . .

BRIDESMAID

Address . . . .

Phone (home) (   ) . . . . (work) (   ) . . . .

Responsibilities . . . .

Parties/events to attend . . . .

Travel/arrival plans . . . .

Lodging . . . .

. . . .

GROOMSMAN

Address . . . .

. . . .

Phone (home) (   ) . . . .   (work) (   ) . . . .

Responsibilities . . . .

. . . .

Parties/events to attend . . . .

. . . .

Travel/arrival plans . . . .

. . . .

Lodging . . . .

. . . .

. . . .

GROOMSMAN

Address . . . .

. . . .

Phone (home) (   ) . . . .   (work) (   ) . . . .

Responsibilities . . . .

. . . .

Parties/events to attend . . . .

. . . .

Travel/arrival plans . . . .

. . . .

Lodging . . . .

. . . .

. . . .

GROOMSMAN

Address . . . .

. . . .

Phone (home) ( ) . . . . (work) ( ) . . . .

Responsibilities . . . .

. . . .

Parties/events to attend . . . .

. . . .

Travel/arrival plans . . . .

. . . .

Lodging . . . .

. . . .

. . . .

GROOMSMAN

Address . . . .

. . . .

Phone (home) ( ) . . . . (work) ( ) . . . .

Responsibilities . . . .

. . . .

Parties/events to attend . . . .

. . . .

Travel/arrival plans . . . .

. . . .

Lodging . . . .

. . . .

BRIDE'S FAMILY

Name ....

Address ....
....

Phone (home) ( ) .... (work) ( ) ....

Responsibilities ....
....

Parties/events to attend ....
....

Travel/arrival plans ....
....

Lodging ....

Name ....

Address ....
....

Phone (home) ( ) .... (work) ( ) ....

Responsibilities ....
....

Parties/events to attend ....
....

Travel/arrival plans ....
....

Lodging ....

BRIDE'S FAMILY

Name . . . .

Address . . . .

. . . .

Phone (home) (   ) . . . .   (work) (   ) . . . .

Responsibilities . . . .

. . . .

Parties/events to attend . . . .

. . . .

Travel/arrival plans . . . .

. . . .

Lodging . . . .

Name . . . .

Address . . . .

. . . .

Phone (home) (   ) . . . .   (work) (   ) . . . .

Responsibilities . . . .

. . . .

Parties/events to attend . . . .

. . . .

Travel/arrival plans . . . .

. . . .

Lodging . . . .

GROOM'S FAMILY

Name ....

Address ....

....

Phone (home) (   ) .... (work) (   ) ....

Responsibilities ....

....

Parties/events to attend ....

....

Travel/arrival plans ....

....

Lodging ....

Name ....

Address ....

....

Phone (home) (   ) .... (work) (   ) ....

Responsibilities ....

....

Parties/events to attend ....

....

Travel/arrival plans ....

....

Lodging ....

GROOM'S FAMILY

Name ....

Address ....

....

Phone (home) (   ) .... (work) (   ) ....

Responsibilities ....

....

Parties/events to attend ....

....

Travel/arrival plans ....

....

Lodging ....

Name ....

Address ....

....

Phone (home) (   ) .... (work) (   ) ....

Responsibilities ....

....

Parties/events to attend ....

....

Travel/arrival plans ....

....

Lodging ....

OTHER ATTENDANTS

FLOWER GIRL, RING BEARER

Name . . . .

Address . . . .

. . . .

Phone (home) (   ) . . . .   (work) (   ) . . . .

Responsibilities . . . .

. . . .

Parties/events to attend . . . .

. . . .

Travel/arrival plans . . . .

. . . .

Lodging . . . .

Name . . . .

Address . . . .

. . . .

. . . .

Phone (home) (   ) . . . .   (work) (   ) . . . .

Responsibilities . . . .

. . . .

Parties/events to attend . . . .

. . . .

Travel/arrival plans . . . .

. . . .

Lodging . . . .

Attire and Flowers

Attire

THINGS TO REMEMBER

Allow four to six months for a wedding dress and bridesmaids' dresses to be ordered and altered.

If you can't afford the gown of your dreams, look for a local dressmaker or student who could copy it. (I designed and sewed my own gown, which represented an enormous saving.)

Choose a color scheme that is both flattering to you and your attendants and appropriate to the season and type of ceremony. Consider how the colors may be used in the wedding decorations.

If your and/or your attendants' shoes need to be dyed, be sure to allow sufficient time—a week or two—to have it done.

For the groom, a tuxedo purchased now will last for years. If he rents a tuxedo, be sure it is ordered far enough in advance so that fit and accessories can be checked.

Make an appointment for a facial and haircut a week or two before the wedding date, to allow grow-in time.

Schedule a manicure, pedicure, and shampoo and styling for the day before or the morning of the wedding. If your headpiece or veil is difficult to arrange, ask your hairdresser to come to the place where you will be dressing.

Purchase a going-away outfit and trousseau (this is often a gift from the bride's mother).

BRIDAL GOWN

Gown purchased at ....
....

Contact ....
Phone (   ) .... Cost ....
Date ordered .... Deposit paid ....
Delivery/pickup date .... Balance due ....

Fittings ....
....
....

Headpiece/veil purchased at ....
....

Contact ....
Phone (   ) .... Cost ....
Date ordered .... Deposit paid ....
Delivery/pickup date .... Balance due ....

Shoes purchased at ....
....

Contact .... Cost ....
Phone (   ) .... Dyeing cost ....
Delivery/pickup date ....

Lingerie and accessories ....
....

Beauty appointments ....
....

Notes ....
....
....
....

BRIDESMAIDS

Dresses purchased at ....

....

Contact ....

Phone (   ) .... Cost per dress ....

Date ordered .... Deposit paid ....

Delivery/pickup date .... Balance due ....

Fittings ....

....

Headpieces purchased at ....

....

Contact .... Cost per headpiece ....

Phone (   ) .... Delivery/pickup date ....

Shoes purchased at ....

....

Contact .... Cost ....

Phone (   ) .... Dyeing cost ....

Delivery/pickup date ....

Accessories ....

....

....

Notes ....

....

....

....

....

....

....

....

....

GROOM

Outfit from . . . .
. . . .

Contact . . . .

Phone (   ) . . . . Cost . . . .

Date ordered . . . . Deposit paid . . . .

Delivery/pickup date . . . . Balance due . . . .

Items ordered	Sizes
. . . .	. . . .
. . . .	. . . .
. . . .	. . . .
. . . .	. . . .
. . . .	. . . .
. . . .	. . . .
. . . .	. . . .

Alteration/fitting dates . . . .
. . . .

Accessories . . . .
. . . .
. . . .
. . . .
. . . .
. . . .

Notes . . . .
. . . .
. . . .
. . . .
. . . .
. . . .
. . . .
. . . .
. . . .

GROOMSMEN AND USHERS

Outfits from ....

....

Contact ....

Phone (   ) .... Cost per outfit ....

Date ordered .... Deposit paid ....

Delivery/pickup date .... Balance due ....

Items ordered	Sizes
....	....
....	....
....	....
....	....
....	....
....	....
....	....

Alteration/fitting dates ....

....

Accessories ....

....

....

....

....

....

Notes ....

....

....

....

....

....

....

....

....

OTHER MEMBERS OF THE WEDDING PARTY

RING BEARER, FLOWER GIRL

Attire for ....
From ....
....

Contact ....
Phone (   ) .... Cost ....
Date ordered .... Deposit paid ....
Delivery/pickup date .... Balance due ....

Items ordered	Sizes
....	....
....	....
....	....
....	....
....	....
....	....
....	....

Attire for ....
From ....
....

Contact ....
Phone (   ) .... Cost ....
Date ordered .... Deposit paid ....
Delivery/pickup date .... Balance due ....

Items ordered	Sizes
....	....
....	....
....	....
....	....
....	....
....	....
....	....

OTHER MEMBERS OF THE WEDDING PARTY

PARENTS AND GRANDPARENTS

Attire for ....
From ....
....

Contact ....
Phone ( ) .... Cost ....
Date ordered .... Deposit paid ....
Delivery/pickup date .... Balance due ....

Items ordered	Sizes
....	....
....	....
....	....
....	....
....	....
....	....
....	....

Attire for ....
From ....
....

Contact ....
Phone ( ) .... Cost ....
Date ordered .... Deposit paid ....
Delivery/pickup date .... Balance due ....

Items ordered	Sizes
....	....
....	....
....	....
....	....
....	....
....	....
....	....

NOTES AND ESTIMATES

1. Rose bouquet with lilies of the valley

2. Peonies, delphinium, irises in a wicker basket

3. Wildflowers in copper kettles

4. Wildflowers in a wheelbarrow

5. Roses in small bud vases

6. Bouquets of different flowers and in different colors

7. Hybrid tea roses with tuberose, sweet peas, and lilies of the valley

8. Stephanotis blossoms

9. Long-stemmed French tulips

10. Long-stemmed giant Swiss pansies

11. French-braided bouquet with roses

12. Roses, lilies of the valley, blue salvia, and lavender sweet peas

13. Pine bough tied onto a wooden pew

14. White lilacs

15. Baby's breath and roses

2

3

4

5

7

9

8

10

11

12

13

14

15

Flowers

THINGS TO REMEMBER

Choose bouquets and flowers that are appropriate for the time and place of the ceremony. Order boutonnieres or corsages for relatives or people performing special duties at the wedding.

Find out what greenery or flowers are available at the ceremony and reception locations. Ask whether there are any floral restrictions at either location.

Schedule several appointments with your florist. Take pictures of bouquets and arrangements you like. Show the florist a swatch of your dress fabric and a photo of the dress itself, so the flowers can be coordinated. Do the same with the bridesmaids' dresses.

Confirm delivery and setup schedules at both ceremony and reception sites.

Coordinate timing for the arrival of flowers at the appropriate places. Make sure refrigeration is available, if necessary, and that pins are provided.

The florist can decorate the cake knife and/or cake itself with flowers and ribbons, or provide flowers for the caterer.

A special "throwing bouquet" can be ordered if you wish to save your bouquet.

If you provide flowers for the ceremony, arrange for someone to take them home; otherwise, they will be discarded.

MY FAVORITE FLOWERS FOR WEDDING BOUQUETS

Alstromeria

Astilbe

Azaleas

Baby gladiolas

Bachelor buttons

Brodia

Buttercups

Calla lilies

Campanula

Clematis

Curly willow

Daffodils

Dahlias

Daisies

Delphiniums

Eremurus

Ferns

Feverfew

Flax

Freesias

Hemlock

Herbs (allium, bishop's-weed, chives, dill, lamb's ears, physotegia, rosemary, sage, tansy)

Hyacinths

Hybrid grasses

Ixia

Laceflowers

Larkspur

Lilacs

Lilies of the valley

Long-stemmed pansies

Lysianthus

Narcissus

Nerines

Orchids (Cattleya, Dendrobium)

Pansies

Peonies

Pinks

Poppies

Queen Anne's lace

Quince blossoms

Ranunculus

Rhododendrons

Roses

Rubrum lilies

Scabiosa

Schizanthus

Scilla

Smilax

Stars of Bethlehem

Stephanotis

Stock

Sweet peas

Thistles

Tulips

Variegated miniature ivy

Wax flowers

WEDDING PARTY FLOWERS

Florist ....

....

Contact .... Phone (   ) ....

Bride's bouquet ....

....

....

....

.... Cost ....

Maid/matron of honor's bouquet ....

....

....

....

.... Cost ....

Bridesmaids' bouquets ....

....

....

.... Cost ....

Flower girls' baskets ....

....

....

.... Cost ....

Groom's boutonniere ....

....

....

.... Cost ....

Groomsmen's boutonnieres ....

....

....

.... Cost ....

Mothers', grandmothers', sisters' corsages ....

....

....

.... Cost ....

Fathers', grandfathers', brothers' boutonnieres ....

....

....

.... Cost ....

Additional flowers ....

....

....

.... Cost ....

Total cost ....

Deposit .... Balance due ....

Delivery instructions ....

....

....

....

....

....

....

....

....

....

....

....

....

....

....

....

....

....

PRESERVING BOUQUETS

Beautiful flowers are a special part of every wedding, and preserving the bridal bouquet can be a unique and lasting memento. There are several ways to "dry" flowers, but I prefer to use silica gel. This is a powdery, sandlike substance available at nurseries, garden centers, and craft and hardware stores. It absorbs the moisture from flowers in a matter of days, thereby preserving their shapes and allowing their colors to remain clear. Check the gel package for a complete list of the flowers it can be used on.

To dry your flowers, fill an airtight container (a tin or a plastic food container) about ⅓ full with silica gel. Trim the flower stems to a length of 1 inch, and place the flower heads *face up* in the silica gel. Flower stems cannot be dried, as they become too brittle. If you plan to use the flowers in an arrangement, you must wire the cut stems first by pushing a 2-inch piece of florists' wire through the stem. After the flowers have dried, attach an additional piece of wire to whatever length you need.

Press the flowers gently into the silica gel. Slowly pour a bit more silica gel onto each flower, taking care to follow its form. Fill the spaces between the petals to retain the flower's actual shape. Do not let the silica gel flatten the flower head. Continue adding gel until the flowers are completely covered. Close the container. Then check the flowers every day until the blue dots in the mixture turn pink and the petals are dry and crisp. This will take from 2 to 7 days depending upon the thickness of the petals. Do not let the flowers dry out too much or they may "shatter" when touched. Remove the flowers with a slotted spoon and brush off any excess silica gel from the petals with a soft brush.

To re-create your bouquet, attach florists' wire to the short wire now protruding from the 1-inch stem. Wire the flowers together in a bouquet, and add ribbons, lace, or whatever decoration was part of your original bouquet.

Another possibility is to ask your florist to preserve your bouquet. Many florists will do this for a fee.

FLOWERS FOR THE CEREMONY

Simple and subtle aesthetics should prevail at the wedding ceremony so as not to detract from the beauty of the location, the ritual, and the principals. Sprays of flowers, leaves, or ivy can be tied to the pews and candles or single lilies can be positioned along the aisles; garden walkways can be marked with ribbons.

Flowers for ceremony	Cost

Total cost

Schedule of delivery and setup

FLOWERS FOR THE RECEPTION

The cost of flowers can easily (and quickly) escalate. One way to keep it in check is to use your own freshly cut flowers (if possible, plan a cutting garden specifically for this purpose). You can also borrow from meadows (after asking the owners' permission). If you must purchase flowers, use those that are in season—ask your florist what will be available on your wedding date. If you choose potted flowering plants, topiaries, or standards to decorate tables, they can be kept long after the reception is over.

. . . .

Flowers for reception	Cost
. . . .	. . . .
. . . .	. . . .
. . . .	. . . .
. . . .	. . . .
. . . .	. . . .
. . . .	. . . .
. . . .	. . . .
. . . .	. . . .
. . . .	. . . .
. . . .	. . . .
. . . .	. . . .
. . . .	. . . .
. . . .	. . . .
. . . .	. . . .
. . . .	. . . .
. . . .	. . . .
. . . .	. . . .

Total cost . . . .

Schedule of delivery and setup . . . .

. . . .

. . . .

. . . .

. . . .

. . . .

NOTES AND ESTIMATES

Ceremony and Celebrations

Prenuptial Parties

THINGS TO REMEMBER

Prenuptial parties can take many forms: a series of small dinner parties, a large cocktail party to introduce the bride- and groom-to-be to distant family and friends, a luncheon or tea to introduce the wedding parties to each other.

Traditional parties include an engagement party, showers, a bachelor party, a brides-maids' party, and a rehearsal dinner.

If your ceremony and reception are to be small, intimate affairs, you might want to invite business and social acquaintances to celebrate at a party beforehand.

Send a thank-you note (or a small gift or flowers) to the host or hostess, and to the guests if you received gifts from them.

SHOWER

No longer bound to the traditional single-sex shower, hostesses (and hosts) now exercise their imaginations to come up with unique coed party themes. There are gardening showers (plants, equipment, books); bar showers; wine showers, where each guest or couple supplies a favorite bottle of wine for the newlyweds' cellar; and "around-the-clock" showers, where gifts must be appropriate to the hour of day assigned each of the guests (for example, a negligee for the 1:00 A.M. gift, an egg timer for 8:00 A.M.).

. . . .

Shower hosted by . . . .

Place . . . .

. . . .

Date . . . . Time . . . .

Theme . . . .

GUEST	GIFT	THANK-YOU SENT
. . . .	. . . .	. . . .
. . . .	. . . .	. . . .
. . . .	. . . .	. . . .
. . . .	. . . .	. . . .
. . . .	. . . .	. . . .
. . . .	. . . .	. . . .
. . . .	. . . .	. . . .
. . . .	. . . .	. . . .
. . . .	. . . .	. . . .
. . . .	. . . .	. . . .
. . . .	. . . .	. . . .
. . . .	. . . .	. . . .
. . . .	. . . .	. . . .
. . . .	. . . .	. . . .
. . . .	. . . .	. . . .
. . . .	. . . .	. . . .

BRIDESMAIDS' PARTY

The bridesmaids' party is a chance for you to thank your attendants for the time and effort they spent on your wedding, and also for their friendship and support. The form it takes is your choice: a tea party, luncheon at a favorite restaurant, or perhaps a dinner for them and their guests. This party can be given any time during the weeks preceding the wedding. It is a good time to present your bridesmaids with their gifts.

Party given at ....

Date .... Time ....

Guests ....

Menu and beverages ....

OTHER PARTIES

Party hosted by ....

Place ....

....

Date .... Time ....

Guests ....

Party hosted by ....

Place ....

....

Date .... Time ....

Guests ....

THE REHEARSAL

When planning the wedding rehearsal, consider inviting some wedding participants in addition to the members of the wedding party: the musicians, the photographer, and perhaps the caterer. That way, everyone will know what to expect the day of the wedding.

Rehearsal date and time ....

Location ....

Attending ....

Things to rehearse (for example, seating of guests, passing of bouquets, exchange of rings, communion or breaking of glass) ....

Transportation arrangements ....

REHEARSAL DINNER

Although traditionally the groom's family gives the rehearsal dinner, it can, of course, be hosted by anyone. If it is financially and logistically possible, you might invite out-of-town friends and distant relatives with whom you would like to spend time before the often-hectic wedding day.

. . . .

Party hosted by . . . .

Place . . . .

. . . .

Date . . . . Time . . . .

Guests . . . .

Menu and beverages . . . .

Rental equipment . . . .

Decorations . . . .

Rehearsal Dinner Seating Plan

Use this sheet of paper to make a to-scale plan of the arrangement of tables and guests at the rehearsal dinner party. Include table settings, decorations, and lighting.

Please Sign Guest Boo

The Ceremony

THINGS TO REMEMBER

Check availability of dressing rooms at ceremony location.

Find out if the location is available for decorating the day before the ceremony, and what time it will be available the day of the wedding.

Check to be sure there are sufficient parking facilities. If not, make other parking arrangements.

Find out what restrictions there may be regarding candles, flashbulbs, occupancy, throwing of rice, etc.

Find out what equipment, such as chairs, pew markers, or aisle runners, is available, and at what extra cost.

For an outdoor wedding, make alternate plans in the event of bad weather.

Coordinate the rehearsal date with all concerned, confirm the date, and call to remind all the participants.

THE CEREMONY

Ceremony location . . . .

. . . .

Contact . . . .

Phone (   ) . . . . Fee . . . .

Officiant . . . .

Address . . . .

Phone (   ) . . . . Fee . . . .

Officiant . . . .

Address . . . .

Phone (   ) . . . . Fee . . . .

Timing of ceremony (start of music, arrival of guests, arrival of wedding party, vows, readings, exchange of rings, departure time) . . . .

. . . .

. . . .

. . . .

. . . .

. . . .

Special vows, readings, songs, music . . . .

. . . .

. . . .

. . . .

. . . .

. . . .

Order of Processional . . . .

. . . .

. . . .

. . . .

. . . .

. . . .

Order of Recessional ....
....
....
....
....
....

Seating order of guests (traditionally, the bride's family and friends are on the left, the groom's on the right; first rows are reserved for immediate family) ....
....
....
....
....
....

SOME FAVORITE READINGS

Genesis 1:26–28

Genesis 2:18, 21–24

Isaiah 61:10

Hosea 2:19–21

Selections from the Song of Solomon

Proverbs 31:10–31

Ruth 1:16–17

Ecclesiastes 3:1–9

Selections from Psalms

The Beatitudes (Matthew 5:3–12)

Mark 10:6–9

John 15:9–12, 17:22–24

Corinthians 13:1–13

Ephesians 5:1–2, 21–33

Romans 12:1–2, 9–18

I John 3:18–24

Sonnets by Elizabeth Barrett Browning

"Joined for Life" by George Eliot

Sonnets by Shakespeare

WEDDING AND RECEPTION LOCATION

Exceptional locations for weddings can be found in most cities and towns these days. Check with local historical societies or even the chamber of commerce for charming historical buildings in your area that may be available for rental. The local parks-and-recreation department may be able to suggest community-owned properties that can be rented. And don't forget to inquire about rental possibilities at museums, arboretums, formal gardens, and even wineries.

Location

Contact
Phone ( )
Fee
Deposit paid
Balance due

Equipment and service available

Restrictions

Times available

The Reception

THINGS TO REMEMBER

Find out whether the location has restrictions about alcohol, occupancy, tents, etc.

Check whether musicians, caterer, photographer, etc., need approval of location's management.

Check the power supply; you may need a stand-by generator.

Find out whether there are stoves, refrigerators, etc., at the location, and if the caterer will be able to use them.

Make sure parking facilities are sufficient.

Be sure bathroom facilities are sufficient. Request fancy soaps, hand towels, and potpourri, or buy them yourself.

Find out what the cancellation policies are.

If young children and babies will be attending, it would be helpful if you hired a baby-sitter.

If the reception is to be outdoors, spray the yard for insects the day before and again on the morning of the wedding.

Plan for sufficient illumination if the reception will run into the night.

Choose a secure place for guests to leave wedding gifts. Buy a beautiful book for guests to sign (and a pen).

Flowers and decoration preparations.

RECEPTION SCHEDULE

Writing out a timetable, however general, for the reception—noting how much time to allow for the receiving line, what time food will be served, when the first dance will be, the cutting of the cake—will help ensure that the afternoon or evening passes exactly as you want it to. If you distribute copies to all concerned—including the musicians, photographer, and caterer—your wishes and their services can easily be coordinated.

LAYOUT OF GROUNDS AND/OR INTERIORS

Use this sheet of paper to make a to-scale plan (select a scale appropriate to the size of the site). Indicate placement of tables, decorations, lighting, bandstand, bar, cake, service area, etc.

RENTALS

Whether you will handle all rentals for the reception or your caterer will (as is usually the case), a good deal of organization is imperative. You must think not only about what should be ordered, but about quantities; your caterer, and perhaps the rental company, can be helpful in this regard. Confirm whether or not the caterer will wash glasses if necessary. Carefully review the terms of the rental contract—this includes timing and scheduling for setup and breakdown, custodial care, etc. Find out who is responsible for clean-up and trash removal.

Popular rental glass sizes include the 10½-ounce all-purpose stemmed wineglass, the 8-ounce tulip and flute champagne glasses, and the 5-ounce saucer champagne glass. (If your budget is tight, keep in mind that a bottle of champagne will go further served in saucer glasses.) If you want bar glasses—although the 10½-ounce all-purpose suffices nicely—the 11- to 12-ounce square highball and the 11- to 12-ounce double rocks glass are also available.

Rental company . . . .

Contact . . . . Phone ( ) . . . .

Rental items . . . .

. . . .

Rentals to be delivered . . . .

Rentals to be picked up . . . .

Total cost of rentals . . . .

Deposit paid . . . .

Balance due . . . .

Rental company . . . .

Contact . . . . Phone ( ) . . . .

Rental items . . . .

. . . .

Rentals to be delivered . . . .

Rentals to be picked up . . . .

Total cost of rentals . . . .

Deposit paid . . . .

Balance due . . . .

Rental Checklist

. . . .

Q T Y T A B L E S

. . . . Round 24″. . .48″. . .54″. . .60″. . .72″. . .

. . . . Long 4 ft . . . 6 ft . . . 8 ft . . .

. . . . Special

. . . .

Q T Y C H A I R S

. . . . Style

. . . .

Q T Y L I N E N

. . . . Round size . . . Color . . .

. . . . Long size . . . Color . . .

. . . . Square size . . . Color . . .

. . . . Liners

. . . . Kitchen white linen

. . . . Napkins . . . Color . . .

. . . . Paper napkins . . . Color . . .

. . . . Waiter serving napkins

. . . . Kitchen towels

. . . . Aprons, full

. . . .

Q T Y C H I N A

. . . . Pattern . . .

. . . . Soup bowl

. . . . Liner

. . . . Bread/butter

. . . . Luncheon

. . . . Dinner

. . . . Cake plate

. . . . Compote

. . . . Bowls

. . . . Coffee cups/saucers

. . . . Demitasse cups/saucers

. . . .

Q T Y S I L V E R W A R E

. . . . Pattern . . .

. . . . Salad fork

. . . . Salad knife

. . . . Fish knife

. . . . Dinner fork

. . . . Dinner knife

. . . . Butter spreaders

. . . . Soup spoon

. . . . Cake fork

. . . . Dessert spoon

. . . . Teaspoon

. . . . Demitasse spoon

. . . . Serving fork/spoon sets

. . . .

Q T Y B A R W A R E

. . . . Glass pitchers

. . . . Ice tubs

. . . . Plastic or carpet runners

. . . . Glass bowls

. . . . Plastic glasses

QTY GLASSWARE

.... All-purpose bar

.... Wine, 10½-oz. red . . . 8-oz. white . . .

.... Goblet, 15-oz.

.... Water (stem)

.... Tulip champagne

.... Flute champagne

.... Saucer champagne

.... Highball

.... Double rocks

.... Mugs

.... Snifter

....

QTY TRAYS

.... Lucite

.... Lacquered

.... Round silver 12″ . . . 14″ . . . 16″ . . .

.... 15 x 20 oval meat platter

.... Vegetable bowls, silver

.... Vegetable bowls, glass

.... Vegetable bowls, Lucite

....

QTY KITCHEN

.... Proofer, tall

.... Proofer, short

.... Proofer trays

.... Sterno

.... BBQ grill

.... Charcoal

.... Cutting boards (cheese)

.... Chafers. . . Size

.... Waiters' stands/trays

.... Trash barrels/liners

....

QTY ACCESSORIES

.... Coffee maker 35 . . . 50 . . . 100 . . . cups

.... Coffee servers, silver

.... Samovar (. . . cups)

.... Cream/sugar. . . Silver/glass. . .

.... Salt/pepper sets

.... Punch bowl/ladle

.... Table numbers/stands

.... Votive candles/holders

.... Ashtrays

.... Silent butlers

.... Coat racks

.... Hangers/numbers

.... Folding screens

....

QTY MISC.

....

....

TENTS

In addition to tents themselves, tent rentals often include dance floors, bandstands, Astroturf, space heaters, roll-down sides, portable toilets, and sometimes tables and chairs. Check with your tent rental company.

. . . .

Tent rental company . . . .

. . . .

Contact . . . . Phone (   ) . . . .

Rental items	Cost
. . . .	. . . .
. . . .	. . . .
. . . .	. . . .
. . . .	. . . .
. . . .	. . . .
. . . .	. . . .
. . . .	. . . .
. . . .	. . . .
. . . .	. . . .
. . . .	. . . .
. . . .	. . . .
. . . .	. . . .

Total cost . . . .

Deposit paid . . . .

Balance due . . . .

Setup schedule . . . .

. . . .

. . . .

Breakdown schedule . . . .

. . . .

. . . .

LIGHTING

Lighting frequently evolves as the final decorative element in a wedding, but at a reception that lingers into nightfall it is very important, and should be given serious thought. Ask friends, and perhaps the tent rental company, for referrals to lighting specialists; then ask to see portfolios or examples of their work. Lighting can take many forms: special effects, balloon lighting, or spot lighting, for example. Elegant table lamps, hurricane lamps, candelabra, votive candles, or torches can also be used, and are often lovely alternatives to professional lighting.

. . . .

Lighting company . . . .

. . . .

Contact . . . . Phone ( ) . . . .

Lighting needed	Cost
. . . .	. . . .
. . . .	. . . .
. . . .	. . . .
. . . .	. . . .
. . . .	. . . .
. . . .	. . . .
. . . .	. . . .
. . . .	. . . .

Total cost . . . .
Deposit paid . . . .
Balance due . . . .

Setup schedule . . . .

. . . .

. . . .

Breakdown schedule . . . .

. . . .

. . . .

Transportation

Things to Remember

Arrange transportation for the bride and groom's parents from the ceremony to the reception so the receiving line won't be held up.

If necessary, help out-of-town guests with transportation by arranging rides for them with friends or other guests.

Make sure the drivers are aware of scheduling details; a schedule should be supplied to each one.

The car the wedding couple will ride in should have a very roomy backseat, which is best for a voluminous gown.

Driving services will often provide experienced drivers to act as parking valets.

CEREMONY AND RECEPTION

Besides the traditional limousine, there are many other ways to transport the wedding party to the ceremony and reception. For a unique alternative (especially for the bride and groom), consider hiring a horse and carriage, an antique Rolls-Royce, a London taxi, a horse-drawn sleigh, a hot-air balloon, or a jet ski. For guests, investigate old-fashioned school buses, a parade of carriages, or even a Greyhound.

. . . .

Transportation service . . . .

. . . .

Contact . . . .

Phone (   ) . . . .

Number of cars, drivers needed . . . .

Fee . . . .

Deposit paid . . . .

Balance due . . . .

Tips . . . .

Transportation to/from wedding rehearsal and rehearsal dinner . . . .

. . . .

. . . .

. . . .

. . . .

. . . .

. . . .

. . . .

. . . .

Transportation to ceremony for . . . .

. . . .

. . . .

. . . .

. . . .

. . . .

. . . .

Pickup

Directions

Ceremony at

Order of vehicles to ceremony

Order of vehicles leaving ceremony

Directions to reception

Transportation leaving reception

NOTES AND ESTIMATES

Just Married !

Catering and Services

1. Orange-Almond Cake with Grand Marnier Italian Meringue Buttercream

2. Wedding Spice Cake with Grand Marnier Italian Meringue Buttercream

3. Orange-Almond Cake with Grand Marnier Italian Meringue Buttercream

4. Basketweave Cake with Handmade Sugar-dough Flowers

5. Whipped-cream Cake with Grand Marnier Italian Meringue Buttercream

6. Chocolate Ganache Groom's Cake

7. Jane Stacey's Hazelnut Genoise and Dacquoise Wedding Cake

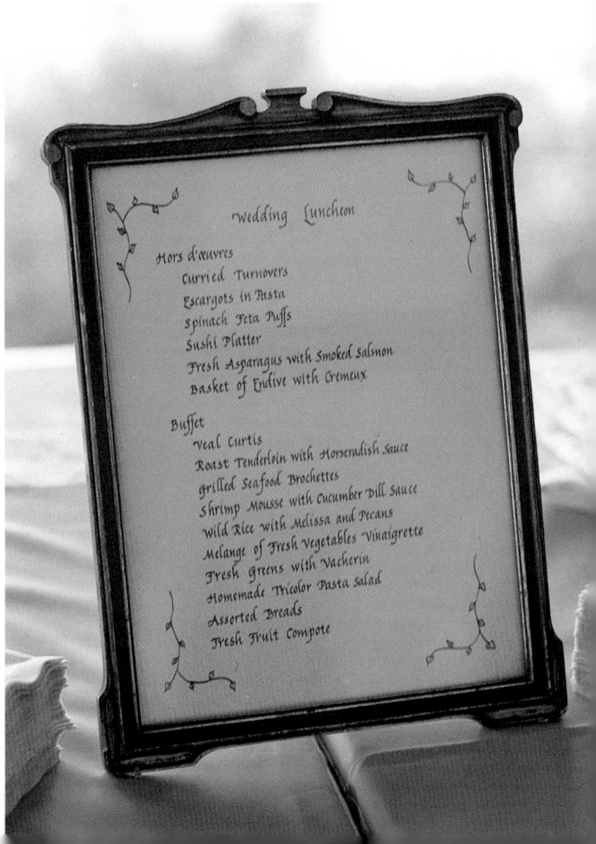
Wedding Luncheon
Hors d'œuvres
Curried Turnovers
Escargots in Pasta
Spinach Feta Puffs
Sushi Platter
Fresh Asparagus with Smoked Salmon
Basket of Endive with Cremeux
Buffet
Veal Curtis
Roast Tenderloin with Horseradish Sauce
Grilled Seafood Brochettes
Shrimp Mousse with Cucumber Dill Sauce
Wild Rice with Melissa and Pecans
Melange of Fresh Vegetables Vinaigrette
Fresh Greens with Vacherin
Homemade Tricolor Pasta Salad
Assorted Breads
Fresh Fruit Compote

2

1

3

4

5

6

7

Food and Beverages

THINGS TO REMEMBER

Decide whether to include the photographer, musicians, rental space, and catering staffs in guest count (i.e., will the caterer be feeding them?).

Let the caterer know the final guest count at least one week before the wedding. Find out what the cancellation policy is.

Include tax and tips in the estimate for caterer.

Check caterer's contract to see who is responsible for breakage of rental items.

If the caterer handles rentals, is there a service charge?

Check on staff attire.

For the bar setup, you will need ice, napkins, bar fruits, etc. For the cake, you'll need a knife and tray. Make sure a staff person is assigned to cut the cake, and to save any leftover cake (especially the top layer).

FOOD

The time of day, the place, and the style of a reception are the most important factors to consider when deciding upon a menu. A late-morning ceremony might suggest a brunch, beginning with light hors d'oeuvres and Bloody Marys, or champagne and peach nectar, followed by eggs Benedict on artichoke bottoms, spicy apple pancakes, and an array of smoked fish and homemade breads. After a noon wedding, a simple buffet luncheon might include several fresh salads and an elegant poached fish. For an afternoon or early-evening reception, an array of hors d'oeuvres and a well-laden fruit-and-cheese table would be appropriate. A dinner reception can be buffet or sit-down, as elegant and many-coursed, or as simple, as you wish. You can even extend the menu with a dessert buffet.

Caterer ....

Contact .... Phone (   ) ....

Number of guests ....

Menu ....

Special menu requests ....

Food garnishes ....

Food cost per person . . . .

Number of service staff, duties . . . .

Service staff cost per hour . . . .

Minimum/overtime . . . .

Dress of service staff . . . .

Arrival/setup time . . . .

Scheduled departure time . . . .

Schedule . . . .

Special responsibilities . . . .

THE CATERER

It is important to hire the right caterer for your needs and for the style of your wedding, and to establish a comfortable and trusting working relationship. The best way to find the right caterer is probably by recommendation. Or think of the best party you've ever been to and find out who was responsible. Ask to see photos from parties the caterer has done, so you know how the food will look. If a restaurant is catering the event, be sure to eat there beforehand to see what the food and service are like. Estimates from two or three caterers will help you compare price and creativity of menus. If you have a specific menu in mind (Oriental, vegetarian), make sure the caterer can create it.

Check the contract carefully for provisions regarding responsibilities, timing (arrival and departure), financial arrangements, staffing, and the supply of foodstuffs and materials.

. . . .

Caterer/Restaurant . . . .

. . . .

Contact . . . . Phone (   ) . . . .

Number of guests . . . . Food cost per person . . . .

Sample menu . . . .

. . . .

. . . .

. . . .

. . . .

Will special menu/dietary requests be available? . . . .

Number of service staff, duties . . . .

. . . .

Service staff cost per hour (if restaurant, tips/service charge included?) . . . .

. . . .

If restaurant, is a private room available (extra charge?)? . . . .

. . . .

THE WEDDING CAKE

The centerpiece of any wedding feast is, of course, the wedding cake—and this is how it always has been. Recently, however, it has become *de rigueur* to have a delicious cake as well as a beautiful one. Wedding cakes are no longer just for show—they are meant to be eaten and enjoyed. And so the standard white cake has given way to carrot, spice, lemon, hazelnut, and even chocolate cakes, although the icing generally remains white.

It is still customary to save the top layer of the wedding cake and eat it on the first anniversary for continued luck. This layer should be removed before the cake is cut. It must be well wrapped in several layers of plastic wrap before freezing.

. . . .

Cake baker . . . .

. . . .

Contact . . . . Phone (   ) . . . .

Cost . . . .

Deposit paid . . . .

Balance due . . . .

Description of cake(s) . . . .

. . . .

. . . .

. . . .

. . . .

. . . .

Delivery instructions . . . .

. . . .

. . . .

Special responsibilities . . . .

. . . .

. . . .

. . . .

. . . .

. . . .

BEVERAGES

On the average, you should allow 1 drink per person per hour at the reception. Depending on the time of day, type of reception, and season of the year, however, your needs may vary—the number of drinks per hour may be higher in warm weather, and people generally drink more in the evening. Ask your beverage supplier or caterer for their expert advice. To help you estimate quantities, you should know that:

1 bottle wine	= 5–6 partially filled glasses	1 liter liquor	= 25 drinks
1 bottle champagne	= 5–6 partially filled glasses	1.75 liters liquor	= 45 drinks
		23 ounces Perrier	= 4 servings
		½ keg beer	= 260 8-ounce glasses

When purchasing beverages, remember that it is much better to err on the side of generosity—and most reputable dealers will accept the return of unopened bottles. (Be sure the staff is under strict orders not to open bottles unnecessarily—they should wait until a bottle is finished before opening another one.) Don't forget to have enough nonalcoholic beverages or a refreshing punch on hand as well.

When setting up a bar, keep in mind that plastic tubs or pails are best for chilling beverages, as they prevent leakage and staining. Cubes are much easier to use for chilling than block ice. Speaking of ice, allow 1 pound per person in hot weather, less in cold, and order extra for chilling. Check on whether the reception site has facilities for chilling beverages and, if so, whether deliveries can be made ahead of time.

. . . .

Beverage supplier . . . .

Contact . . . . Phone (   ) . . . .

To be supplied . . . . Cost . . . .

. . . . Deposit paid . . . .

. . . . Balance due . . . .

. . . . Delivery instructions . . . .

. . . .

. . . .

. . . .

Returns agreement . . . .

Beverage supplier ....

Contact .... Phone (   ) ....

To be supplied .... Cost ....
.... Deposit paid ....
.... Balance due ....
.... Delivery instructions ....
....
....

Returns agreement ....

Beverage supplier ....

Contact .... Phone (   ) ....

To be supplied .... Cost ....
.... Deposit paid ....
.... Balance due ....
.... Delivery instructions ....
....
....

Returns agreement ....

Beverage supplier ....

Contact .... Phone (   ) ....

To be supplied .... Cost ....
.... Deposit paid ....
.... Balance due ....
.... Delivery instructions ....
....
....
....

Returns agreement ....

NOTES AND ESTIMATES

Music

THINGS TO REMEMBER

Before you hire musicians, go to hear them play or listen to a tape to be certain they are right for your wedding.

Check on musical restrictions at ceremony and reception sites.

Check electrical outlets—you may need more power from a rented generator.

Decide where to locate the musicians for best effect.

Check attire of the musicians.

Decide how you want to handle toasts, cake cutting, tossing of bouquet, etc. If you want special music to announce these events, write out a schedule for the musicians to follow.

Make a list of requested songs and send it to the musicians ahead of time.

MUSIC FOR CEREMONY

Musician(s) . . . .

. . . .

. . . .

. . . .

Contact . . . . Phone (   ) . . . .

Fee . . . .

Deposit paid . . . .

Balance due . . . .

Arrival/starting time . . . .

Requested music . . . .

. . . .

. . . .

. . . .

. . . .

. . . .

. . . .

. . . .

. . . .

. . . .

Playing schedule . . . .

. . . .

. . . .

. . . .

. . . .

. . . .

. . . .

. . . .

. . . .

. . . .

. . . .

. . . .

. . . .

MUSIC FOR RECEPTION

Musician(s) ....

....

....

....

Contact .... Phone (   ) ....

Fee ....

Deposit paid ....

Balance due ....

Arrival/departure time ....

Requested music ....

....

....

....

....

....

....

....

....

....

Playing schedule ....

....

....

....

....

....

....

....

....

....

....

....

POPULAR WEDDING MUSIC

PROCESSIONALS

Bridal Chorus from *Lohengrin* (Wagner)

Trumpet Voluntary in D Flat (Jeremiah Clarke)

Selections from *The Water Music* (Handel)

Processional in G Major (Handel)

Adagio in A Minor (Bach)

Jesu, Joy of Man's Desiring (Bach)

Sheep May Safely Graze (Bach)

Canon in D Major (Pachelbel)

Wedding March from *The Marriage of Figaro* (Mozart)

Wachet auf (Bach)

Ave Maria (Schubert or Verdi)

Traditional Hebrew love songs

Settings of "Dodi li" (I Am My Beloved's) and "Havana Babanof" (Beautiful One)

RECESSIONALS

Wedding March from *A Midsummer Night's Dream* (Mendelssohn)

Crown Imperial March (Sir William Walton)

"Ode to Joy" from the Ninth Symphony (Beethoven)

Toccata from Organ Symphony No. 5 (Charles Marie Widor)

Trumpet Tune in C (Purcell)

Postlude in G Major (Handel)

Photography and Video Services

THINGS TO REMEMBER

Formal portraits for newspapers must usually be taken far in advance of wedding day.

Check on restrictions regarding use of cameras, lights, and flash. In many churches and synagogues, photography is not allowed during the ceremony.

Check on staff attire—at a formal wedding, photography staff should be dressed in black tie; at an informal wedding they should wear dark suits so as not to stand out from the guests.

Make a list of photos you want taken: people, events, and settings (buffet table, cake table, or flower arrangements, for example).

Ask friends to bring cameras and supply you with copies of their photos; you will get a great selection of shots that have a different feeling from that of the professional photographer.

PHOTOGRAPHY

Photography is one of the most important elements of your wedding, for after the day is over, it is all that will remain. Photographs will supplement your memories of the day. Use care when selecting a photographer or a video service—ask for recommendations from your friends, and look at portfolios or tapes. Scrutinize the person's ability to capture the moments you want captured: does he/she work best with candids or posed photos? In black-and-white or color? Choose someone whose sensibility you like.

The contract should be very clear on all matters, including the unforeseen (and unfortunate): for example, if the photographer's camera breaks down at the wedding, you will be glad you required that a second camera must be available. Specify in writing who selects the photographs you will pay for. The contract should permit you to see contact sheets and negatives, and to have a say in what photos are selected. (Better yet, see if you can buy the negatives outright.) Confirm arrival and departure times so that nothing is missed by the camera.

If your budget is a concern, don't forget to investigate local art schools—their photography students may be perfect for your needs.

. . . .

FORMAL PORTRAITS

Photographer . . . .

. . . .

Contact . . . . Phone (   ) . . . .

Fee . . . .

Deposit paid . . . .

Balance due . . . .

Appointment schedule . . . .

. . . .

. . . .

. . . .

. . . .

. . . .

Photographs to be seen . . . . delivered . . . .

CEREMONY/RECEPTION PHOTOGRAPHS

Photographer . . . .

. . . .

Contact . . . . Phone (   ) . . . .

Fee . . . .

Deposit paid . . . .

Balance due . . . .

Number of prints/photos/slides . . . .

Arrival/departure times . . . .

. . . .

. . . .

People, places, events to photograph . . . .

. . . .

. . . .

. . . .

. . . .

. . . .

. . . .

. . . .

. . . .

. . . .

. . . .

. . . .

. . . .

. . . .

. . . .

. . . .

. . . .

. . . .

. . . .

Photographs to be seen . . . . delivered . . . .

VIDEO SERVICES

Videos are an increasingly important part of a wedding's documentation, but they are not the most important part. Make it clear to the video team that they should stay in the background at all times and not make themselves obtrusive, especially at the more solemn moments. If you hire both a photographer and a video team, make sure they realize they are there for different reasons and that you don't want any competition between them.

Don't reject the idea of a home video taken by a competent relative or close friend if you can't afford a professional—it can also preserve the memory.

Ask to see a rough edit of the video, and be sure the contract allows you to eliminate any segments you don't like and have a say in the final look of the video. Make sure the accompanying music supplied by the video team is to your liking.

. . . .

Video service . . . .

. . . .

Contact . . . . Phone (   ) . . . .

Fee . . . .

Deposit paid . . . .

Balance due . . . .

Tapes to be delivered . . . .

Arrival/departure times . . . .

Events, places to videotape . . . .

. . . .

. . . .

. . . .

. . . .

. . . .

. . . .

. . . .

. . . .

. . . .

. . . .

Guests and Gifts

Mr. William Sylvester Cargill
and
Mr. and Mrs. Harris Edward Russell
request the honour of your presence
at the marriage of their daughter
Martha Lynne
Mr. and Mrs. Lionel Tomerlin
request the pleasure of your company
at the marriage of their daughter
Mr. John Hayden Crawford
on Saturday the first of June

Celebrate with us!
a wedding reception for Rochelle and Doug
Sunday, June 15, 1980, 2 p.m., informal
Love Nadya and Dick
Will Attend
Will Not Attend

Patrice Moser & Boyd Morrison
Invitation
Wedding
We graciously request
the pleasure of
your company
for the celebration of
our wedding day.
Saturday
The twenty-ninth of August
Nineteen hundred and eighty-seven
Half past one o'clock in the afternoon
The Wedding Pa
Patrice Angela Moser
Bride
Maria Moser Ghoneim
Matron of Honor
James Coleman Butler
Best Man
Elizabeth Schrafft Moser
Mother of the Bride
Pamela Rosser Morrison
Mother of the Groom
Sarah Elizabeth Ghone
Melissa Morriton Pe
Répondez S'il Vous Plaît
Will attend
Will not attend
Name(s)
Please reply by August 2nd, 1987
Highlands
LONG BRANCH
Long Branch
Red Bank
Little Silver
Shrewsbury
Fair Haven
Rumson
Asbury Park
Ocean Grove
Bradley Beach
Belmar
Spring Lake
Sea Girt
Manasquan
Pt. Pleasant Beach
Point Pleasant
Candlewood
Brookwood
Gael Towey & Stephen Doyle
invite you to their wedding
Saturday the sixteenth of
May nineteen hundred
at the Connell
house, Sea Girt, New Jersey.
R S V P
FIELD CONVOLVULUS.
CHARLES
AND
MARY LOUISE
MELCHIOR
REQUEST THE PLEASURE
OF YOUR COMPANY
AT
THE WEDDING OF THEIR DAUGHTER
JEANNE
TO
CHRISTOPHER SCHULTZ
DAY, FEBRUARY 15, 1988
4:00 P.M.
FRIENDS MEETING
& CHESTER AVENUE
NEW JERSEY
TAVERN
STREET
NEW JERSEY
JANUARY 20, 1988

Invitations and Stationery

THINGS TO REMEMBER

Engraved invitations can take four weeks or more to print, and should therefore be ordered eight to ten weeks before the wedding.

Order more invitations than you think you will need; the extras can be used for last-minute invitations, for correcting mistakes, and as keepsakes.

You may be able to get the envelopes before the invitations, so you can begin addressing them immediately.

Invitations should be mailed four to six weeks before the wedding, or even earlier to guests who live out of town and will need to make arrangements for transportation and accommodation.

Buy romantic or otherwise appropriate stamps.

Order other stationery and paper items at the same time: place cards, pew cards, announcements, at-home cards, response cards, napkins, matches, thank-you notes.

INVITATIONS

Engraved invitations (or announcements) are no longer the rule of the day. Museum cards with handwritten notes may suffice for small, informal weddings; personalized invitations can be designed by artist friends; or elegantly handwritten invitations can be offset on good-quality stationery. It is nicest if the invitation reflects your personality and the style of your wedding. If you want to use a calligrapher—for either the invitations themselves or to address envelopes—ask at art schools or local adult-education centers.

. . . .

Stationer . . . .

. . . .

Contact . . . . Phone (   ) . . . .

Invitation style, quantity ordered . . . .

. . . .

Delivery date . . . . Cost . . . .

Other items ordered . . . . Deposit paid . . . .

. . . . Balance due . . . .

OTHER STATIONERY

. . . .

. . . .

. . . .

. . . .

. . . .

. . . .

. . . .

. . . .

. . . .

. . . .

. . . .

. . . .

Guest List

Things to Remember

Soon after the wedding date has been chosen, the parents of the bride and groom should be asked to prepare lists of the family and friends they wish to invite. Combine these with your own lists, and make an estimate of the expected responses and the number you expect to attend in each party.

Make a special note of guests who live out of town and plan to send them (with their invitations) maps, parking information, and transportation schedules.

Arrange moderately priced accommodations, if possible, for out-of-town guests. Reserve a block of rooms at a convenient hotel so guests can attend functions together, sharing cabs and rides. Ask for a group rate.

If you do not receive an RSVP within a week or two of the wedding, have a representative of the bride (the maid/matron of honor, or the bride's mother) call to see if the invited guest will attend.

Keep an up-to-date list of gifts as they arrive, and send thank-yous promptly.

GIFT REGISTRY

To make gift-giving easier, many stores have gift registries where a bride-to-be registers for items she would like to receive for her home. This practice ensures that the couple will receive at least some things they really need and want. Guests can ask the bride's family where she is registered.

Store

Contact Phone ( )

Registered for

Store

Contact Phone ( )

Registered for

INVITATION LIST AND GIFTS RECEIVED

Name ....
Address ....
Phone (   ) .... Number attending ....
Gift, store .... Thank-you sent ....

Name ....
Address ....
Phone (   ) .... Number attending ....
Gift, store .... Thank-you sent ....

Name ....
Address ....
Phone (   ) .... Number attending ....
Gift, store .... Thank-you sent ....

Name ....
Address ....
Phone (   ) .... Number attending ....
Gift, store .... Thank-you sent ....

Name ....
Address ....
Phone (   ) .... Number attending ....
Gift, store .... Thank-you sent ....

Name ....
Address ....
Phone (   ) .... Number attending ....
Gift, store .... Thank-you sent ....

Name ....
Address ....
Phone (   ) .... Number attending ....
Gift, store .... Thank-you sent ....

Name . . . .
Address . . . .
Phone (   ) . . . . Number attending . . . .
Gift, store . . . . Thank-you sent . . . .

Name . . . .
Address . . . .
Phone (   ) . . . . Number attending . . . .
Gift, store . . . . Thank-you sent . . . .

Name . . . .
Address . . . .
Phone (   ) . . . . Number attending . . . .
Gift, store . . . . Thank-you sent . . . .

Name . . . .
Address . . . .
Phone (   ) . . . . Number attending . . . .
Gift, store . . . . Thank-you sent . . . .

Name . . . .
Address . . . .
Phone (   ) . . . . Number attending . . . .
Gift, store . . . . Thank-you sent . . . .

Name . . . .
Address . . . .
Phone (   ) . . . . Number attending . . . .
Gift, store . . . . Thank-you sent . . . .

Name . . . .
Address . . . .
Phone (   ) . . . . Number attending . . . .
Gift, store . . . . Thank-you sent . . . .

Name
Address
Phone ( )
Number attending
Gift, store
Thank-you sent

Name
Address
Phone ( )
Number attending
Gift, store
Thank-you sent

Name
Address
Phone ( )
Number attending
Gift, store
Thank-you sent

Name
Address
Phone ( )
Number attending
Gift, store
Thank-you sent

Name
Address
Phone ( )
Number attending
Gift, store
Thank-you sent

Name
Address
Phone ( )
Number attending
Gift, store
Thank-you sent

Name
Address
Phone ( )
Number attending
Gift, store
Thank-you sent

Name ....

Address ....

Phone (   ) .... Number attending ....

Gift, store .... Thank-you sent ....

Name ....

Address ....

Phone (   ) .... Number attending ....

Gift, store .... Thank-you sent ....

Name ....

Address ....

Phone (   ) .... Number attending ....

Gift, store .... Thank-you sent ....

Name ....

Address ....

Phone (   ) .... Number attending ....

Gift, store .... Thank-you sent ....

Name ....

Address ....

Phone (   ) .... Number attending ....

Gift, store .... Thank-you sent ....

Name ....

Address ....

Phone (   ) .... Number attending ....

Gift, store .... Thank-you sent ....

Name ....

Address ....

Phone (   ) .... Number attending ....

Gift, store .... Thank-you sent ....

Name . . . .
Address . . . .
Phone (   ) . . . . Number attending . . . .
Gift, store . . . . Thank-you sent . . . .

Name . . . .
Address . . . .
Phone (   ) . . . . Number attending . . . .
Gift, store . . . . Thank-you sent . . . .

Name . . . .
Address . . . .
Phone (   ) . . . . Number attending . . . .
Gift, store . . . . Thank-you sent . . . .

Name . . . .
Address . . . .
Phone (   ) . . . . Number attending . . . .
Gift, store . . . . Thank-you sent . . . .

Name . . . .
Address . . . .
Phone (   ) . . . . Number attending . . . .
Gift, store . . . . Thank-you sent . . . .

Name . . . .
Address . . . .
Phone (   ) . . . . Number attending . . . .
Gift, store . . . . Thank-you sent . . . .

Name . . . .
Address . . . .
Phone (   ) . . . . Number attending . . . .
Gift, store . . . . Thank-you sent . . . .

Name ....
Address ....
Phone (   ) .... Number attending ....
Gift, store .... Thank-you sent ....

Name ....
Address ....
Phone (   ) .... Number attending ....
Gift, store .... Thank-you sent ....

Name ....
Address ....
Phone (   ) .... Number attending ....
Gift, store .... Thank-you sent ....

Name ....
Address ....
Phone (   ) .... Number attending ....
Gift, store .... Thank-you sent ....

Name ....
Address ....
Phone (   ) .... Number attending ....
Gift, store .... Thank-you sent ....

Name ....
Address ....
Phone (   ) .... Number attending ....
Gift, store .... Thank-you sent ....

Name ....
Address ....
Phone (   ) .... Number attending ....
Gift, store .... Thank-you sent ....

Name . . . .
Address . . . .
Phone ( ) . . . . Number attending . . . .
Gift, store . . . . Thank-you sent . . . .

Name . . . .
Address . . . .
Phone ( ) . . . . Number attending . . . .
Gift, store . . . . Thank-you sent . . . .

Name . . . .
Address . . . .
Phone ( ) . . . . Number attending . . . .
Gift, store . . . . Thank-you sent . . . .

Name . . . .
Address . . . .
Phone ( ) . . . . Number attending . . . .
Gift, store . . . . Thank-you sent . . . .

Name . . . .
Address . . . .
Phone ( ) . . . . Number attending . . . .
Gift, store . . . . Thank-you sent . . . .

Name . . . .
Address . . . .
Phone ( ) . . . . Number attending . . . .
Gift, store . . . . Thank-you sent . . . .

Name . . . .
Address . . . .
Phone ( ) . . . . Number attending . . . .
Gift, store . . . . Thank-you sent . . . .

Name

Address

Phone (   ) Number attending

Gift, store Thank-you sent

Name

Address

Phone (   ) Number attending

Gift, store Thank-you sent

Name

Address

Phone (   ) Number attending

Gift, store Thank-you sent

Name

Address

Phone (   ) Number attending

Gift, store Thank-you sent

Name

Address

Phone (   ) Number attending

Gift, store Thank-you sent

Name

Address

Phone (   ) Number attending

Gift, store Thank-you sent

Name

Address

Phone (   ) Number attending

Gift, store Thank-you sent

Name ....
Address ....
Phone (   ) .... Number attending ....
Gift, store .... Thank-you sent ....

Name ....
Address ....
Phone (   ) .... Number attending ....
Gift, store .... Thank-you sent ....

Name ....
Address ....
Phone (   ) .... Number attending ....
Gift, store .... Thank-you sent ....

Name ....
Address ....
Phone (   ) .... Number attending ....
Gift, store .... Thank-you sent ....

Name ....
Address ....
Phone (   ) .... Number attending ....
Gift, store .... Thank-you sent ....

Name ....
Address ....
Phone (   ) .... Number attending ....
Gift, store .... Thank-you sent ....

Name ....
Address ....
Phone (   ) .... Number attending ....
Gift, store .... Thank-you sent ....

Name ....
Address ....
Phone (   ) .... Number attending ....
Gift, store .... Thank-you sent ....

Name ....
Address ....
Phone (   ) .... Number attending ....
Gift, store .... Thank-you sent ....

Name ....
Address ....
Phone (   ) .... Number attending ....
Gift, store .... Thank-you sent ....

Name ....
Address ....
Phone (   ) .... Number attending ....
Gift, store .... Thank-you sent ....

Name ....
Address ....
Phone (   ) .... Number attending ....
Gift, store .... Thank-you sent ....

Name ....
Address ....
Phone (   ) .... Number attending ....
Gift, store .... Thank-you sent ....

Name ....
Address ....
Phone (   ) .... Number attending ....
Gift, store .... Thank-you sent ....

Name . . . .
Address . . . .
Phone ( ) . . . . Number attending . . . .
Gift, store . . . . Thank-you sent . . . .

Name . . . .
Address . . . .
Phone ( ) . . . . Number attending . . . .
Gift, store . . . . Thank-you sent . . . .

Name . . . .
Address . . . .
Phone ( ) . . . . Number attending . . . .
Gift, store . . . . Thank-you sent . . . .

Name . . . .
Address . . . .
Phone ( ) . . . . Number attending . . . .
Gift, store . . . . Thank-you sent . . . .

Name . . . .
Address . . . .
Phone ( ) . . . . Number attending . . . .
Gift, store . . . . Thank-you sent . . . .

Name . . . .
Address . . . .
Phone ( ) . . . . Number attending . . . .
Gift, store . . . . Thank-you sent . . . .

Name . . . .
Address . . . .
Phone ( ) . . . . Number attending . . . .
Gift, store . . . . Thank-you sent . . . .

Name ....
Address ....
Phone ( ) .... Number attending ....
Gift, store .... Thank-you sent ....

Name ....
Address ....
Phone ( ) .... Number attending ....
Gift, store .... Thank-you sent ....

Name ....
Address ....
Phone ( ) .... Number attending ....
Gift, store .... Thank-you sent ....

Name ....
Address ....
Phone ( ) .... Number attending ....
Gift, store .... Thank-you sent ....

Name ....
Address ....
Phone ( ) .... Number attending ....
Gift, store .... Thank-you sent ....

Name ....
Address ....
Phone ( ) .... Number attending ....
Gift, store .... Thank-you sent ....

Name ....
Address ....
Phone ( ) .... Number attending ....
Gift, store .... Thank-you sent ....

Name . . . .
Address . . . .
Phone (   ) . . . . Number attending . . . .
Gift, store . . . . Thank-you sent . . . .

Name . . . .
Address . . . .
Phone (   ) . . . . Number attending . . . .
Gift, store . . . . Thank-you sent . . . .

Name . . . .
Address . . . .
Phone (   ) . . . . Number attending . . . .
Gift, store . . . . Thank-you sent . . . .

Name . . . .
Address . . . .
Phone (   ) . . . . Number attending . . . .
Gift, store . . . . Thank-you sent . . . .

Name . . . .
Address . . . .
Phone (   ) . . . . Number attending . . . .
Gift, store . . . . Thank-you sent . . . .

Name . . . .
Address . . . .
Phone (   ) . . . . Number attending . . . .
Gift, store . . . . Thank-you sent . . . .

Name . . . .
Address . . . .
Phone (   ) . . . . Number attending . . . .
Gift, store . . . . Thank-you sent . . . .

Name . . . .
Address . . . .
Phone (   ) . . . .   Number attending . . . .
Gift, store . . . .   Thank-you sent . . . .

Name . . . .
Address . . . .
Phone (   ) . . . .   Number attending . . . .
Gift, store . . . .   Thank-you sent . . . .

Name . . . .
Address . . . .
Phone (   ) . . . .   Number attending . . . .
Gift, store . . . .   Thank-you sent . . . .

Name . . . .
Address . . . .
Phone (   ) . . . .   Number attending . . . .
Gift, store . . . .   Thank-you sent . . . .

Name . . . .
Address . . . .
Phone (   ) . . . .   Number attending . . . .
Gift, store . . . .   Thank-you sent . . . .

Name . . . .
Address . . . .
Phone (   ) . . . .   Number attending . . . .
Gift, store . . . .   Thank-you sent . . . .

Name . . . .
Address . . . .
Phone (   ) . . . .   Number attending . . . .
Gift, store . . . .   Thank-you sent . . . .

Name . . . .
Address . . . .
Phone ( ) . . . . Number attending . . . .
Gift, store . . . . Thank-you sent . . . .

Name . . . .
Address . . . .
Phone ( ) . . . . Number attending . . . .
Gift, store . . . . Thank-you sent . . . .

Name . . . .
Address . . . .
Phone ( ) . . . . Number attending . . . .
Gift, store . . . . Thank-you sent . . . .

Name . . . .
Address . . . .
Phone ( ) . . . . Number attending . . . .
Gift, store . . . . Thank-you sent . . . .

Name . . . .
Address . . . .
Phone ( ) . . . . Number attending . . . .
Gift, store . . . . Thank-you sent . . . .

Name . . . .
Address . . . .
Phone ( ) . . . . Number attending . . . .
Gift, store . . . . Thank-you sent . . . .

Name . . . .
Address . . . .
Phone ( ) . . . . Number attending . . . .
Gift, store . . . . Thank-you sent . . . .

Name . . . .
Address . . . .
Phone (   ) . . . .   Number attending . . . .
Gift, store . . . .   Thank-you sent . . . .

Name . . . .
Address . . . .
Phone (   ) . . . .   Number attending . . . .
Gift, store . . . .   Thank-you sent . . . .

Name . . . .
Address . . . .
Phone (   ) . . . .   Number attending . . . .
Gift, store . . . .   Thank-you sent . . . .

Name . . . .
Address . . . .
Phone (   ) . . . .   Number attending . . . .
Gift, store . . . .   Thank-you sent . . . .

Name . . . .
Address . . . .
Phone (   ) . . . .   Number attending . . . .
Gift, store . . . .   Thank-you sent . . . .

Name . . . .
Address . . . .
Phone (   ) . . . .   Number attending . . . .
Gift, store . . . .   Thank-you sent . . . .

Name . . . .
Address . . . .
Phone (   ) . . . .   Number attending . . . .
Gift, store . . . .   Thank-you sent . . . .

Name ....
Address ....
Phone (   ) .... Number attending ....
Gift, store .... Thank-you sent ....

Name ....
Address ....
Phone (   ) .... Number attending ....
Gift, store .... Thank-you sent ....

Name ....
Address ....
Phone (   ) .... Number attending ....
Gift, store .... Thank-you sent ....

Name ....
Address ....
Phone (   ) .... Number attending ....
Gift, store .... Thank-you sent ....

Name ....
Address ....
Phone (   ) .... Number attending ....
Gift, store .... Thank-you sent ....

Name ....
Address ....
Phone (   ) .... Number attending ....
Gift, store .... Thank-you sent ....

Name ....
Address ....
Phone (   ) .... Number attending ....
Gift, store .... Thank-you sent ....

Name ....
Address ....
Phone (   ) .... Number attending ....
Gift, store .... Thank-you sent ....

Name ....
Address ....
Phone (   ) .... Number attending ....
Gift, store .... Thank-you sent ....

Name ....
Address ....
Phone (   ) .... Number attending ....
Gift, store .... Thank-you sent ....

Name ....
Address ....
Phone (   ) .... Number attending ....
Gift, store .... Thank-you sent ....

Name ....
Address ....
Phone (   ) .... Number attending ....
Gift, store .... Thank-you sent ....

Name ....
Address ....
Phone (   ) .... Number attending ....
Gift, store .... Thank-you sent ....

Name ....
Address ....
Phone (   ) .... Number attending ....
Gift, store .... Thank-you sent ....

Name ....

Address ....

Phone (   ) .... Number attending ....

Gift, store .... Thank-you sent ....

Name ....

Address ....

Phone (   ) .... Number attending ....

Gift, store .... Thank-you sent ....

Name ....

Address ....

Phone (   ) .... Number attending ....

Gift, store .... Thank-you sent ....

Name ....

Address ....

Phone (   ) .... Number attending ....

Gift, store .... Thank-you sent ....

Name ....

Address ....

Phone (   ) .... Number attending ....

Gift, store .... Thank-you sent ....

Name ....

Address ....

Phone (   ) .... Number attending ....

Gift, store .... Thank-you sent ....

Name ....

Address ....

Phone (   ) .... Number attending ....

Gift, store .... Thank-you sent ....

Name ....
Address ....
Phone (   ) .... Number attending ....
Gift, store .... Thank-you sent ....

Name ....
Address ....
Phone (   ) .... Number attending ....
Gift, store .... Thank-you sent ....

Name ....
Address ....
Phone (   ) .... Number attending ....
Gift, store .... Thank-you sent ....

Name ....
Address ....
Phone (   ) .... Number attending ....
Gift, store .... Thank-you sent ....

Name ....
Address ....
Phone (   ) .... Number attending ....
Gift, store .... Thank-you sent ....

Name ....
Address ....
Phone (   ) .... Number attending ....
Gift, store .... Thank-you sent ....

Name ....
Address ....
Phone (   ) .... Number attending ....
Gift, store .... Thank-you sent ....

Name ....
Address ....
Phone (   ) .... Number attending ....
Gift, store .... Thank-you sent ....

Name ....
Address ....
Phone (   ) .... Number attending ....
Gift, store .... Thank-you sent ....

Name ....
Address ....
Phone (   ) .... Number attending ....
Gift, store .... Thank-you sent ....

Name ....
Address ....
Phone (   ) .... Number attending ....
Gift, store .... Thank-you sent ....

Name ....
Address ....
Phone (   ) .... Number attending ....
Gift, store .... Thank-you sent ....

Name ....
Address ....
Phone (   ) .... Number attending ....
Gift, store .... Thank-you sent ....

Name ....
Address ....
Phone (   ) .... Number attending ....
Gift, store .... Thank-you sent ....

ANNOUNCEMENT LIST

Name ....
Address ....
....
....

Name ....
Address ....
....
....

Name ....
Address ....
....
....

Name ....
Address ....
....
....

Name ....
Address ....
....
....

Name ....
Address ....
....
....

Name ....
Address ....
....
....

Name ....
Address ....
....
....

Name ....
Address ....
....
....

Name ....
Address ....
....
....

Name ....
Address ....
....
....

Name ....
Address ....
....
....

Name ....
Address ....
....
....

Name ....
Address ....
....
....

Name ....

Address ....

....

....

Name ....

Address ....

....

....

Name ....

Address ....

....

....

Name ....

Address ....

....

....

Name ....

Address ....

....

....

Name ....

Address ....

....

....

Name ....

Address ....

....

....

Name ....

Address ....

....

....

Name ....

Address ....

....

....

Name ....

Address ....

....

....

Name ....

Address ....

....

....

Name ....

Address ....

....

....

Name ....

Address ....

....

....

Name ....

Address ....

....

....

Name ....

Address ....

....

....

Name ....

Address ....

....

....

Name ....
Address ....
....
....

Name ....
Address ....
....
....

Name ....
Address ....
....
....

Name ....
Address ....
....
....

Name ....
Address ....
....
....

Name ....
Address ....
....
....

Name ....
Address ....
....
....

Name ....
Address ....
....
....

Name ....
Address ....
....
....

Name ....
Address ....
....
....

Name ....
Address ....
....
....

Name ....
Address ....
....
....

Name ....
Address ....
....
....

Name ....
Address ....
....
....

Name ....
Address ....
....
....

Name ....
Address ....
....
....

OTHER GIFTS

From . . . .
Address . . . .
. . . .
Gift, store . . . .
Thank-you sent . . . .

From . . . .
Address . . . .
. . . .
Gift, store . . . .
Thank-you sent . . . .

From . . . .
Address . . . .
. . . .
Gift, store . . . .
Thank-you sent . . . .

From . . . .
Address . . . .
. . . .
Gift, store . . . .
Thank-you sent . . . .

From . . . .
Address . . . .
. . . .
Gift, store . . . .
Thank-you sent . . . .

From . . . .
Address . . . .
. . . .
Gift, store . . . .
Thank-you sent . . . .

From . . . .
Address . . . .
. . . .
Gift, store . . . .
Thank-you sent . . . .

From . . . .
Address . . . .
. . . .
Gift, store . . . .
Thank-you sent . . . .

From . . . .
Address . . . .
. . . .
Gift, store . . . .
Thank-you sent . . . .

From . . . .
Address . . . .
. . . .
Gift, store . . . .
Thank-you sent . . . .

From . . . .
Address . . . .
. . . .
Gift, store . . . .
Thank-you sent . . . .

From . . . .
Address . . . .
. . . .
Gift, store . . . .
Thank-you sent . . . .

From . . . .
Address . . . .
. . . .
Gift, store . . . .
Thank-you sent . . . .

From . . . .
Address . . . .
. . . .
Gift, store . . . .
Thank-you sent . . . .

From . . . .
Address . . . .
. . . .
Gift, store . . . .
Thank-you sent . . . .

From . . . .
Address . . . .
. . . .
Gift, store . . . .
Thank-you sent . . . .

From . . . .
Address . . . .
. . . .
Gift, store . . . .
Thank-you sent . . . .

From . . . .
Address . . . .
. . . .
Gift, store . . . .
Thank-you sent . . . .

From . . . .
Address . . . .
. . . .
Gift, store . . . .
Thank-you sent . . . .

From . . . .
Address . . . .
. . . .
Gift, store . . . .
Thank-you sent . . . .

From . . . .
Address . . . .
. . . .
Gift, store . . . .
Thank-you sent . . . .

From . . . .
Address . . . .
. . . .
Gift, store . . . .
Thank-you sent . . . .

From . . . .
Address . . . .
. . . .
Gift, store . . . .
Thank-you sent . . . .

From . . . .
Address . . . .
. . . .
Gift, store . . . .
Thank-you sent . . . .

From . . . .
Address . . . .
. . . .
Gift, store . . . .
Thank-you sent . . . .

From . . . .
Address . . . .
. . . .
Gift, store . . . .
Thank-you sent . . . .

ACCOMMODATIONS FOR OUT-OF-TOWN GUESTS

If you have reserved rooms for out-of-towners, ask for clear, foolproof directions from the hotel staff and enclose a copy in the invitation, or send it after you have received a response. Find out if a shuttle service from major transportation terminals is offered, and let people know.

Although the bride usually makes the hotel reservations, the guests assume payment of the bill.

. . . .

Hotel . . . .

. . . .

Contact . . . . Rates . . . .

Phone . . . . Reservation deadline . . . .

Directions . . . .

. . . .

. . . .

GUESTS	DATES NEEDED	ROOM NUMBER
. . . .	. . . .	. . . .
. . . .	. . . .	. . . .
. . . .	. . . .	. . . .
. . . .	. . . .	. . . .
. . . .	. . . .	. . . .
. . . .	. . . .	. . . .
. . . .	. . . .	. . . .
. . . .	. . . .	. . . .
. . . .	. . . .	. . . .
. . . .	. . . .	. . . .
. . . .	. . . .	. . . .
. . . .	. . . .	. . . .
. . . .	. . . .	. . . .
. . . .	. . . .	. . . .

GUESTS	DATES NEEDED	ROOM NUMBER

OUT-OF-TOWN GUESTS

If you have guests coming from out of town, it would be thoughtful to inform them of airline and train schedules to your location (enclosed, perhaps, with the wedding invitation), and to have your travel agent help with their reservations. Try also to arrange transportation to the ceremony and reception for them with friends, relatives, other guests.

. . . .

Transportation needed for out-of-town guests . . . .

Honeymoon

The Honeymoon

THINGS TO REMEMBER

Accomplish as much as possible in the weeks before the wedding: shop, exchange money, buy travelers' checks; pack, etc.

Buy or borrow any luggage you need (good luggage is a wonderful wedding present).

Make sure passports and visas are in order; keep them with your tickets and remember where they are so you won't be searching frantically at the last minute.

If you leave for your honeymoon immediately after the reception, ask your maid of honor or a family member to catalog and hold the wedding presents until you return.

Allow time after the reception to change and rest before leaving for your honeymoon.

TRAVEL PLANS

Travel agent . . . .

. . . .

Phone ( ) . . . .

Agent/contact at destination . . . . Phone ( ) . . . .

Tickets, passports located . . . .

Itinerary

LOCATION	ARRIVAL	DEPARTURE	ADDRESS, PHONE
. . . .	. . . .	. . . .	. . . .
. . . .	. . . .	. . . .	. . . .
. . . .	. . . .	. . . .	. . . .
. . . .	. . . .	. . . .	. . . .

Accommodations

Hotel . . . .

. . . .

Manager/contact . . . . Phone ( ) . . . .

Reservation/confirmation number . . . .

Check-in, check-out times . . . .

Daily rate . . . .

Special arrangements (car rental, meal plans, etc.) . . . .

. . . .

. . . .

. . . .

. . . .

Credit card numbers . . . .

. . . .

Travelers' check numbers . . . .

. . . .

Hotel . . . .

. . . .

Manager/contact . . . . Phone ( ) . . . .

Reservation/confirmation number . . . .

Check-in, check-out times . . . .

Daily rate . . . .

Special arrangements (car rental, meal plans, etc.) . . . .

. . . .

. . . .

. . . .

. . . .

Credit card numbers . . . .

. . . .

Travelers' check numbers . . . .

. . . .

Hotel . . . .

. . . .

Manager/contact . . . . Phone ( ) . . . .

Reservation/confirmation number . . . .

Check-in, check-out times . . . .

Daily rate . . . .

Special arrangements (car rental, meal plans, etc.) . . . .

. . . .

. . . .

. . . .

. . . .

Credit card numbers . . . .

. . . .

Travelers' check numbers . . . .

. . . .

HONEYMOON TROUSSEAU

A bride's trousseau was originally a grand, final gift to a daughter from her parents. It was a complete wardrobe, intended to see her through the first year of married life, when the young couple was just getting started and would not have much money. Few brides today will acquire such bounty, but all will buy or receive some new clothing: a going-away outfit for the honeymoon, lingerie and nightgowns, or even a piece of good luggage.

Travel Checklist *

Tickets	Alarm clock	First-aid kit	Hair ornaments
Passport	Radio	Medications	Hair dryer
Driver's license	Cassette player	Contraceptives	Razor
Travelers' checks	Cassettes	Tampons	Blades
Credit cards	Camera	Manicure kit	Deodorant
Local currency	Lenses	Cosmetics	Moisturizer
Maps	Film	Toothbrush	Q-tips
Guide books	Lead-lined bag	Toothpaste	Cotton balls
Dictionary	Flashlight	Dental floss	Sun screen
Stationery	Nightlight	Mouthwash	Insect repellent
Memo pads	Batteries	Soap	Room spray
Stamps	Current adaptor	Washcloth	Sunglasses
Diary	Travel iron	Shower cap	Eyeglasses
Address book	Sewing kit	Shampoo	Contact lenses
Pens	Scissors	Conditioner	Lens solution
Pencils	Tweezers	Hairspray	Rubber bands
Calculator	Swiss-army knife	Hairbrush	Plastic bags

P.S. Don't forget good novels and, in case you didn't eat much at the reception, an elegant going-away basket complete with champagne to toast your new life.

* List from Helen and Richard Brandt.